MY YEAR IN VIET NAM

by

John F. Welch

Air Liaison Officer/

Forward Air Controller

in

Viet Nam

July 1966 to July 1967

MY YEAR IN VIET NAM

John F. Welch

Copyright © 2005
All Rights Reserved
Silver Wings Aviation, Inc.
2933 Country Club Drive
Rapid City, SD 57702-5218

USA

ISBN
0-9637909-2-7

Library of Congress Control Number: 2004099802

TABLE OF CONTENTS

	Page No.
FOREWORD	5
ACKNOWLEDGMENTS	5
DEDICATION	6
PROLOGUE	7
CHAPTER I HOW DID I GET INTO THIS MESS?	15
CHAPTER II " OH SHOW ME THE WAY TO--"	19
CHAPTER III WELL, HERE I AM	29
CHAPTER IV LEARNING THE ROPES	33
CHAPTER V QUI NHON-TEMPORARILY	37
CHAPTER VI QUI NHON FOR REAL	49
CHAPTER VII GETTING DOWN TO WORK	63
CHAPTER VIII THE WAR SPEEDS UP	69
CHAPTER IX OPERATION IRVING	91
CHAPTER X THE STRUGGLE GOES ON	109
CHAPTER XI MORE HELP ARRIVES!	115
CHAPTER XII THE HOLIDAYS	125
CHAPTER XIII 1967 WAS HERE!	133

CHAPTER XIV THE CHINESE NEW YEAR--TET!	147
CHAPTER XV DOWN HILL FROM NOW ON?	157
CHAPTER XVI DOWN WHERE THE PEOPLE LIVED	173
CHAPTER XVII R & R TO HONG KONG	191
CHAPTER XVIII BACK TO WORK AGAIN	201
CHAPTER XIX ILLNESS	209
CHAPTER XX TERRORISM, VIET CONG STYLE	217
CHAPTER XXI END OF TOUR REPORT	221
CHAPTER XXII MISCELLANY	225
CHAPTER XXIII FINISHING THE TOUR	231

Foreword

This book is a very personal account of my participation in events in the 1960's which were shaping far ranging consequences to literally millions of people around the Earth. I could not influence happenings on the world's larger stage, but tried to help my hosts, a people I came to love, respect and honor as true patriots of their country.

This is an effort to refresh my own memories, and those of others who served in Viet Nam, of those eventful days, and to offer a viewpoint not widely popular in the United States then, nor even now, more than thirty-seven years later.

Much of this narrative is based on letters I wrote home to my wife, they serve as my Journal for the time. Fortunately for this report, she saved them.

Dates may be fuzzy, actions sometimes seemed to overlap, but at least the larger events are in sequence. Like almost every other person serving there, I kept track of the days in country, and the days yet to go before return to the "good ol' USA".

In 1944, it had been by combat missions flown, rather than by the calendar.

ACKNOWLEDGMENTS

The 1963 Edition of ENCYCLOPEDIA BRITANNICA and its subsequent Books of the Year were referred to for some historical and biographical data in the Prologue.

Dedication

This recital of events is dedicated to the ordinary people of the Republic of Viet Nam, who believed in freedom and fought for it, through many labors, dangers and hardships, and to those of other nations who contributed to their struggle for a chance to control their own destiny. It is a tribute, too, to Viet Nam's hospitality to those who came to help them.

It is especially dedicated to the memory of those very many patriotic Vietnamese who gave their lives in their heroic struggle for freedom, and to the memory of those of the USA and of other nations who also sacrificed their lives, for the same worthy cause.

PROLOGUE

Looking back fifty-some years, we observe a very stressful time in the history of the world, particularly in Southeast Asia. Peaceful peoples were trying to achieve their dream of being able to feed themselves and live in harmony with each other and their neighbors. But an ideology hatched in the other side of the Earth nearly a hundred years earlier was driving into their part of the world from the North. Our special interest is in a land known as Viet Nam.

Communism was at the height of its power. Its mother den was in the Soviet Union, which had destroyed millions of its own people, and had succeeded in capturing the government of the most populous country on earth, China, as well as many others.

Power was what it was all about. No one was to be allowed to oppose its self-appointed leaders, who went to extremes of cruelty and terrorism to wrest any vestige of independence and freedom from the people under their control. To spread this malignancy, the system was on a continual lookout for persons who could be converted to a totalitarian way of thinking, and who would use any means, including terrorism, imprisonment, torture and death, to achieve their ends of complete control of governments and people, and to maintain themselves as the sole rulers. An apt student of this program was a gentleman called (eventually) Ho Chi Minh.

We'll come back to him.

Just a week before Japan surrendered at the end of World War II, two days after the atomic bomb was dropped on Hiroshima, the Soviet Union declared war on Japan. When Japan surrendered a week later, the allies agreed that the Japanese forces north of the 38th parallel across Korea would surrender to the Soviets, and those south of it would surrender to the US. Then, in the interim peace settlement, Korea was artificially and arbitrarily divided at the 38th Parallel, between Soviet control and US influence. The Soviets sealed off the boundary, and refused to let the North participate in free elections to unite the country under one government. The elections were held in South

Korea in 1948. The South became the Republic of Korea, the North was declared the Democratic People's Republic of Korea.

When the United Nations was formed, a seat on the Security Council was assigned to China, at that time under the leadership of Chiang Kai Shek. After the Nationalist Chinese were forced off the mainland, to Taiwan, the Soviet Union claimed that Red China should have the China seat on the UN Security Council. From the beginning of the UN, the USSR had vetoed a number of Council proposed actions. Finally, in protest over the China seat, the USSR delegation walked out of the Council, temporarily taking away its veto of Council actions.

Looking around the world in 1948, President Truman and his Secretary of Defense, Johnson, decided there was no great threat against peace anywhere, and concluded that the US Armed Forces could safely be reduced. So the Army, the Navy and the newly formed Air Force were reduced in numbers by sending many men home. (Some Air Force officers, to continue building time for retirement, enlisted in the lower ranks. They referred to themselves as having been "Johnsonized").

Truman's decision and subsequent actions looked to the Communist world like Opportunity Knocking. It seemed clear to potential aggressors that they would not be opposed by the US. So, on June 25, 1950, while the Soviet walkout was still in effect, the North Korean Army marched South, overcoming the defending forces in the South easily. President Truman immediately committed troops to help the South.

The UN Security Council met, and, unopposed by a veto by the Soviet Union, demanded that North Korea remove its troops from South Korea.

North Korea did not comply, and the UN voted to support its resolution by calling on all its members to support the South with materiel and troops.

The first American troops sent into battle in Korea were ill prepared to fight. They were mostly administrative, motor pool and other support personnel from the Occupation Troops in Japan, without any combat infantry training.

Seventeen nations had troops in the country supporting

the South by the end of 1952, and many others provided medical and other assistance. After much hard fighting, many casualties and two years of negotiations, a truce agreement was reached and signed on July 27, 1953. It essentially restored the 38th parallel as the boundary between North and South, and the truce remains in contentious effect as this is written more than fifty years later. Meanwhile, the South has thrived, with a stable democratic government and a strong economy, while the North has built a big army, developed missiles, and starved its people.

The French established a presence in Indochina in the late 1700's, playing various roles in the area. They intervened more actively during persecutions of Christians in the late 1800's, and remained engaged in Indochina into World War II. During World War II, the Japanese cooperated with the Vichy French, then threw them out of Indochina in March, 1945. After the War, the new French government reasserted its prerogatives in that part of the world, but was opposed by the Vietminh. (See later). It was agreed at the Potsdam conference that Northern Viet Nam would be administered by the Chinese, and the South by the British and the French.

Back to Ho Chi Minh.

Nguyen Tat Tan was born in Kim Lien, in central Viet Nam, in 1890. He early on began revolutionary activities in various areas, and moved to London during World War I. As Nguyen Al Quoc, he went to France as a dock worker in 1919, where he joined the French Communist Party. From there he moved to Moscow, and was fully indoctrinated into Communist philosophy. A short assignment took him to the Soviet Consul's office in Canton. He returned to Moscow, then went to Thailand to help set up an insurrection in Indochina, by forming a Vietnam Workers Party, the Vietminh; it was banned by the French. By now he was known as Ho Chi Minh (the brilliant one).

After the Japanese surrender in 1945, Ho proclaimed the People's Republic of Viet Nam, with himself as president. At first he agreed with the French to make Viet Nam an independent unit in the Indochinese Federation, but his Vietminh began fighting the French in 1946. An extended war finally led to a disastrous defeat of the French at Dien Bien Phu, in 1954. A peace conference in Geneva ensued, participated in by France, the United Kingdom, the US, the USSR, China, North and South Viet Nam, Laos and Cambodia. The People's Republic of Viet Nam, capital in Hanoi, and the Republic of Viet Nam, capital in Saigon, were the outcome, the first of November, 1954. The boundary between the two was established as the Ben-Hai river, near the 17th Parallel. No military troops from other nations were to be allowed in the two countries. Elections to unite the North and the South were to be held in 1956, to reunite the two Viet Nams.

Deja vu, Korea?

Those elections were never held.

The South was glad to be rid of the French, but did not want the Communists. They were joined by 800,000 refugees from the North who agreed with them. The South's economy was in shambles, and its government had to contend with various rebellious factions, some of them religious groups.

Ho Chi Minh had plans to make Viet Nam all one country. There were already Communist agents in the South, and more were sent, to recruit more members to the cause. They became the Viet Cong. Their mission was to eliminate the persons in leadership positions in the South, by kidnapping, assassination or any other means, to create a vacuum of leadership, which the Communists could then fill in. Targeted were hamlet, village, District and Province chiefs, and anyone who was well educated, including doctors, teachers and religious leaders. Finally, no one would allow himself to be elected as Province Chief; to do so was to invite assassination. One result was that most of the Province Chiefs were ARVN (Army of the Republic of Viet Nam) Commissioned Officers, ordered to take their jobs by the central government.

There was also the threat of an invasion by Ho Chi Minh's government, and VC guerilla bands in the South became more active, attacking villages, local defensive forces, and ARVN units. One of their methods of recruiting troops was to take over a hamlet, then draft all its younger male inhabitants into the Viet

Cong. Quite often, when the young men got word the VC were coming, they'd fade away into the jungle. " Draft dodgers"?

A series of changes in the South's government followed, marked by much disagreement about who should lead the country. Ngo Dinh Diem ended up in charge.

Worth noting--Ho Chi Minh's and his successors' objective was always to conquer the South. The South never wanted to take over North Viet Nam, although taking Hanoi was proposed as a solution for ending the fighting.

Meanwhile, the Communist attacks, launched from jungle and other areas, threatened the South's control and defense of its citizens. The South asked for help, and quite a number of nations responded, including the US, the Philippines, Thailand, South Korea, Australia and New Zealand, all of which sent military and civilian advisors, and much financial and materiel aid. The VC expanded its operations, and US Military dependents were sent back to the US for their own safety, while the US Military Advisors got more involved in actual combat. Their tour in Viet Nam was established at one year.

The Vietnamese copilot on one of the early C-47 missions was Col. Nguyen Cao Ky. He was supposed to be in training, but probably was already proficient--he demonstrated a successful landing on a very short runway after his American instructor had missed the approach and gone around twice. Ky was also a graduate of the US Command and General Staff College. He later commanded the VNAF (Viet Nam Air Force).

In November, 1963, Diem was assassinated and his regime was overthrown. Another series of government changes ensued.

During the Viet Nam War, the primary source of manpower for the US Armed Forces was the Selective Service, the Draft. Every able bodied American young man was subject to it. Perhaps most opposed to it were college students.

Some young men elected to enlist in the Service of their choice; some enrolled in Advanced ROTC, which would delay their going into service, and make them commissioned officers upon entry on active duty. Some men joined the National Guard, some the Coast Guard, some enrolled in military flight training.

My Year in Viet Nam

Some simply left the country. How different from 1942!

The greatest successes of the world wide Communist propaganda program of the 1960's were in the US, among college students, the college faculties, and the media--television, radio, movie studios, news magazines and daily newspapers. There were demonstrations against US participation in the Viet Nam War, on college campuses, and in the major cities, often instigated by resident Communist agents. Hardly ever were Allied successes in the field in Viet Nam reported favorably in the media. There were no big welcomes home for individuals or groups of men returning from their year in Viet Nam. Instead they were often greeted with hostility, spat upon, and called baby killers, instead of being honored as the true patriots which most of them were.

In early August, 1964, North Vietnamese naval torpedo boats attacked US Naval vessels in the Gulf of Tonkin, and on August 7, Congress passed the Gulf Of Tonkin Resolution. President Johnson ordered retaliatory air strikes, which severely damaged the North's patrol boat installations, and sank a number of their boats. The US expanded military forces in South Viet Nam, and increased bombing in North Viet Nam. US aid, and numbers of men sent to Viet Nam, continued to increase in 1965.

Nguyen Cao Ky, who had become commander of the VNAF (Viet Nam Air Force), called for an invasion of the North. That made military good sense--the best defense is a strong offense. Later in the year the military leaders of the South brought about his selection as Premier. He instituted many government reforms, and asked for more US military aid and development aid. General elections were set for 1966.

In February, 1966, President Johnson and Premier Ky met in Honolulu and agreed on joint objectives of defeat of the Viet Cong, eradication of social injustice among the Vietnamese people, and the establishment of true democracy for The Republic of Viet Nam.

That's where I came in.

John F. Welch

My Year in Viet Nam

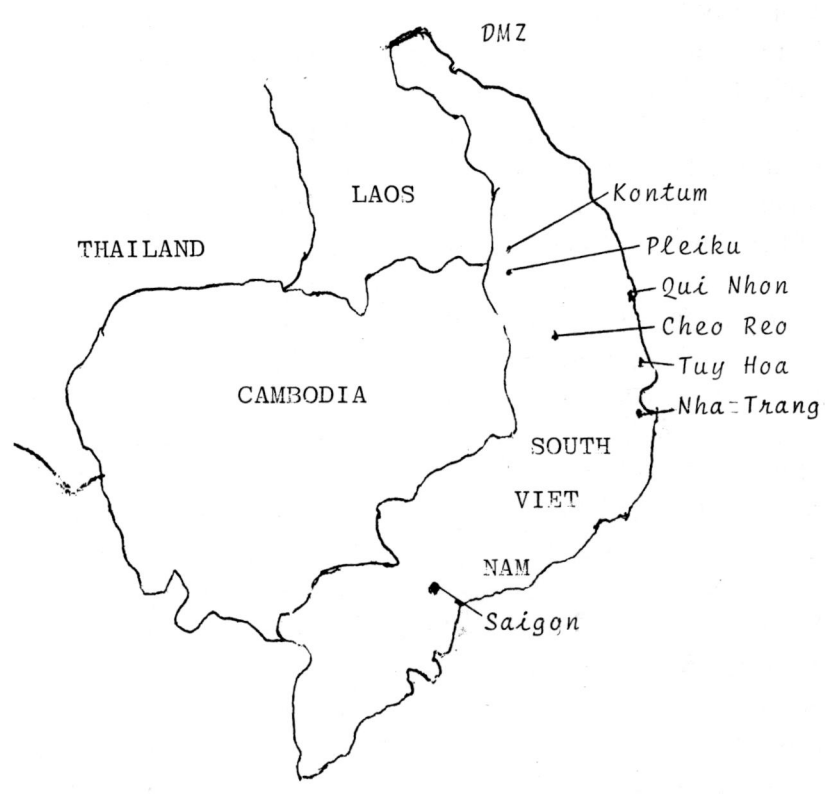

Figure 1.1
   Rough Sketch, Southern Indo Chinese Peninsula

Figure 1.2
A Symbol of an Ancient Land, an Old Chinese Temple

CHAPTER I

HOW DID I GET INTO THIS MESS?

An official looking piece of paper appeared in my In Basket in the B-58 System Program Office at Wright Field one day in the Fall of 1965, so I picked it up and read it. It was from Personnel, saying that I was being changed from Flying Status Code 1-A to Code 1-C, effective February 1, 1966.

It said that since I would complete more than 22 years of flying service in the Air Force in February, and was more than 45 years old, I would be removed from active flying duty, and would no longer maintain flying proficiency as I had been doing with Wright-Patterson Base Operations. Oh, I would still be given Flight Pay, I just wouldn't fly for it.

I picked up the phone and called Personnel.

"What is this business? I joined the Army Air Corps in 1942 to fly. How can they do this to me?"

The nice lady explained that since my job as a Development Engineer didn't require me to fly, and my Unit didn't have any airplanes, the Air Force would save money by not using airplanes to keep me current.

" Well, how can I keep on flying?"

" You would have to be assigned to a job requiring you to fly, in a flying unit," she said.

" What such assignments are available?"

" Come on down to the Office and look at the list," she replied.

I had always wanted to fly big transports, so after looking over the list of possible assignments, I volunteered, on 4 November 1965, for C-133, C-135 and C-141--a fateful move!

Meanwhile I continued my task of completing work on the B-58, wrapping up a fatigue testing program, and getting the contractor started on the development of a Flight Controls System modification--in 1962 a ' 58 had gone sideways at Mach 2, and broken up in flight, killing the crew instantly. We had settled on making the Automatic Flight Control System Triple Redundant.

If the active one of three electronic channels failed, control would switch automatically to one of the two other control channels.

On November 12, I was notified of my selection for a Permanent Change of Station assignment, to a flying position, to occur in the January-June time frame of 1966.

A couple of days after Christmas, the phone rang, and the lady from Personnel said,

" Major Welch, we have an assignment for you."

" Oh, what is it?"

" It says O-1."

" What's an O-1?"

" I don't know what's an O-1," she replied.

She forwarded my Reassignment Order, which said Major John F. Welch had been selected for assignment to the 6250th Combat Support Group (PACAF) APO San Francisco 96307, with TDY en route to attend O-1 Training, Class 66-11, reporting 2 May 1966, Port reporting June 1966.

So I went digging, and discovered that the O-1 had started life as the Army L-19. When I graduated from Kansas State in 1950, I had a job offer from Cessna to help design a new airplane, designated the L-19, that the company had just contracted to build for the US Army. What irony, back after 15 years!

Drafting was not my strong suit, so, instead of going to work for Cessna, I had taken a position as a technical writer at Beech. There I stayed until my Reserve Unit was recalled to Active Duty, for the Korean War, eight months later.

That led to ten years in SAC (Strategic Air Command), five years of experience as a Maintenance Officer, and thousands of pilot flying hours in C-47's, RB-36's and B-52's, nine years of it at Ellsworth AFB, then a year at Sheppard AFB. In early 1961, I finally escaped SAC's clutches, to attend AFIT (the Air Force Institute of Technology) at Wright-Patterson Air Force Base.

My assignment upon graduation in 1962, with a Master of Science Degree in Aeronautical Engineering, was to the B-58 System Program Office, in ASD, to help solve its Flight Control System problems.

Now, I was one of only two persons left there--I had a

secretary. And I had the support of the Engineering Directorates at ASD (Aeronautical Systems Division of Air Force Systems Command). The B-58 System was approaching the final throes of being turned over to Air Force Logistics Command for Materiel support.

My next duty assignment was plain to see. The only places the Air Force was using O-1's were in training at Hurlburt Field, and in Viet Nam. Well, I had asked for it, sort of. And the airplane did have a "1" in its name.

One consolation was that I was not alone; many pilots who had flown nothing but desks for years were being directed back to pilot duties, to take their turns at a year in Viet Nam.

Alberta, my wife of 17 years, wasn't happy about my new assignment. She thought my 35 missions in B-17's in World War Two had been enough of getting shot at--and she was convinced that I had volunteered to be separated from my family for a year, or permanently. Besides, we had a sixteen year old son, a ten year old daughter and a seven year old son who all needed their Dad at home.

The whole family was well attuned to peacetime life in the Air Force. But if one is wearing the blue suit, he goes wherever the Commander-in-Chief sends him, even though he's forty-five, going on forty-six.

Early in January, I was notified of my retention in Flying Status Code 1-A, confirmed by a Personnel Action memo on January 26.

Things then got interesting. A letter on 9 March announced that I'd been selected for promotion to Lt. Colonel. On 10 March, Major John F. Welch received orders to report to Hurlburt Field, Florida, to start combat crew training with Class 66-11B on 16 May, to graduate on 29 June, then proceed to APO SF 96274 for TDY and further transportation to APO SF 96307. (To me, those APO's were mere blobs on the map of the Western Pacific Ocean.)

On 16 March, I was notified that Major John F. Welch's promotion was effective on 20 March 1966. On 24 March, Major John F. Welch's reassignment to 6250th Combat Support Group was rescinded. On 29 March, Lt. Colonel John F. Welch was ordered to report to Hurlburt Field, Florida, to begin training on 16 May with Class 66-11B, etc., etc., etc. I was off the hook, there, for about five days, wasn't I?

A long time friend was also on the Lt. Colonel promotion list, and our wives hosted a party for the two of us at the Officers' Club.

In the interim, I had all kinds of processing to do, including small arms qualification with the .38 Caliber pistol and the M-16 rifle, (I qualified as Expert on both of them), drawing personal equipment, getting shots, and so on.

I also had to get things around the house in shape for a year's absence, and make sure my Personal Affairs were in order. At work, I did the best I could to head the Captain replacing me in the right direction, reveled in a quite complimentary Officer Effectiveness Report, and had a good time at the farewell party in my honor. Preparing the family for my projected absence had its emotional aspects, but we survived. The cars were in good shape, and financial affairs were all arranged.

Was I ready?

CHAPTER II

" OH, SHOW ME THE WAY TO--"

So, on the 13th of May, I tossed my gear in the Studebaker and " lit out" for that suburb of Eglin Air Force Base, Hurlburt Field. There wasn't any space in the VOQ to begin with, so most of Class 66-11B stayed in a local motel just off the Base, for about ten days.

We began our training with ground school. The instructors were O-1 pilots who had completed tours in Viet Nam. All of them were enthusiastic about how well their efforts were appreciated by the folks they had supported, and about the way we were trying to support the Vietnamese.

We learned about the 0-1 Bird Dog's design, performance, and equipment. It had tandem seating for two pilots, with control stick, rudder pedals with brakes, and a left-side mounted throttle quadrant, for each.

Its armament wasn't much. It was equipped with two launching tubes on each wing, switches and circuitry for four 2.75 inch rockets, primarily for white phosphorus target markers. There was no gun sight, the pilot simply aimed the airplane at the target and squeezed the trigger switch. Some pilots found it helpful to use a grease pencil to draw a small circle straight ahead on the windscreen, and then to center the target in it when ready to fire a rocket. Also carried were smoke grenades providing various colors of smoke to aid in marking areas on the ground, and sometimes as signals for visual communications. They were launched by pulling their safety pins, then throwing them out the open side window. Ground forces had them, too.

The airplane was basic, simple. It was a high wing Cessna monoplane, with a single tail, metal fuselage and wings. The landing gear struts were standard Cessna single leaf springs; it had hydraulic brakes, a steerable tail wheel, and a crosswind landing feature. Wing flaps were adjustable to as much as 60 degrees down. The engine was a 230 horsepower six cylinder, horizontal-opposed Continental, de-rated to 215 horsepower, carburetor with mixture control, and dual ignition. The engine was designed for 87 octane fuel, and, burning it, was expected to operate 1700 hours between engine overhauls. The aircraft had excellent short field capability.

It was not intended, or cleared, for aerobatics.

Excellent visibility front, sides, rear and almost straight down was provided by the big windows. Side windows in the doors could be swung out and upward to hook on to the lower wing surfaces. This feature made for better vision to the sides, and allowed air flow through the cabin, much appreciated in hot weather.

The airplane had several radios, VHF, UHF and FM for communications, and ADF for navigation. A special feature of the FM radio, using a whip antenna near each wing tip, made it capable of determining heading directly to or from an FM broadcasting station.

We also studied the climate, terrain, weather, geography, and a little bit about the armed forces of Viet Nam and the Allied Forces we'd be working with. There was also survival information, how to avoid the " bad guys", how to get help from the " good guys", and how to find food and water, if we had to bail out or crash land. We also heard that we'd stop at Clark Field in the Philippines for a special jungle survival course on the way to Viet Nam. It sounded like we'd better be in pretty good physical shape, so several of us started jogging a mile or so every day.

We were also briefed that the supply of O-1's was being used up, and they'd gone out of production years earlier. Procurement had begun on a replacement, the O-2. It was essentially the Cessna Model 337, modified to the armament requirements and radios of the O-1. It was a high-wing twin, with an engine mounted on each end of the cabin, and twin tail booms. I volunteered to try it out if one showed up in my area.

On May 31, flight training began. My assigned instructor was Captain Richard W. Gallop. We got very busy, flying twice on most days, sometimes three. I found the airplane responsive and easy to fly. It simply went where I pointed my nose. There were lots of landings, over 110 in two weeks. Practice forced landings turned out well after I got the proper glide speed figured out, the first time I'd had good forced landing practice since Stearmans in 1943. (Aero Club didn't count). We did two night flights, and I managed to break the tail wheel on one night landing. Gallop thought he did it; I knew I had, but didn't argue the point.

On one target marking practice, directing A-1's on the gunnery range, I managed a direct hit on the target, a burned out truck, with my Willy Pete (White Phosphorus rocket), so I got to tell the fighter pilot,

" Hit my smoke!"

I had one flight in the right seat of an A-1E, an old Navy design, like one of the fighter types we'd be directing in Viet Nam. We started taxiing out with the wings folded, then stopped to extend them and have them checked by ground crew before take off. I surely was hoping they were properly extended and locked! The pilot was also a student getting ready for Viet Nam. He was already " gung ho". On every turn out and up from a dive bombing pass he put my face down almost to between my knees with " g" force. The targets were being marked by some of my classmates.

One of the challenges of the program was to find obscure buildings whose locations were identified by coordinates on an Army map like those used in Viet Nam. They were obscure because they were located in areas of tall trees and did not show up well through the Spanish moss.

As we neared the end of the program, each of us flew on a solo cross country flight to a place of his own choosing, to some distant point. I chose New Orleans. I had a flat tail wheel tire on landing there, and there were no O-1 tail wheel tires at New Orleans. So I had to stay over night waiting for one to be sent in. I decided to take a short cut on return, going direct to Mobile, instead of following Airways, before heading on East to Hurlburt. About the time I got out over all that swamp and water, I began wondering about the wisdom of my choice. Getting ready for SEA?

After another five and a half hours, including a final flight check on June 14, I was deemed qualified, and graduated, with about 35 hours in the O-1. (I'd had a lot more than that in the B-17 than that when we headed overseas in 1944). Anyway, on June 15, I cranked up the Studebaker and reversed course, to our house in Fairborn, Ohio.

My next orders directed me to report not later than 1300 hours 10 July 1966 to the MAC PASSENGER TERMINAL, Travis AFB California, for departure on Flight H243 at 1500 hours 10 July. That gave me some more time to spend with the family.

My travel orders authorized me to take 166 pounds of luggage with me, so when I went to the Military Travel office at Wright-Patterson to get my Airlines Ticket to California, I made sure the extra charge for luggage was included. I dug out my Air Force A-3 and B-4 bags, and packed them. Considering the climate I was going to, I took summer clothing, light weight suit, short sleeve dress shirts, a couple of pairs of light weight trousers, one civilian tie, and of course underwear and socks and handkerchiefs. No heavy underwear! I included two sets of short sleeve summer khakis, no military tie, but did include the flat military cap and uniform insignia. All that, plus my toilet kit, went into the B-4 bag.

Into the A-3 bag went fatigues, flight suits, jungle combat boots, etc. The total in the two bags was substantially less than the authorized 166 pounds, actually only about 80 pounds. I couldn't have carried 166 pounds, anyway.

I found some more things to do around the house. My family would stay in it until my return from Viet Nam.

Finally, on July 8, the family took me to the Dayton Municipal Airport to catch my flight. After teary goodbyes, with everyone being brave, the flight took off for my connecting flight in Cincinnati. That one took off on time, first stop, Dayton(!!), then Indianapolis. Next stop was Chicago. Just as in the heyday of the railroads, all air routes went through Chicago. The flight arrived in San Francisco at 0150 and I caught the scheduled bus, arriving at Fairfield/Travis AFB at 0600. The VOQ was full, so I took a taxi to a nearby motel. A room opened at the VOQ about noon, so I went back there and checked in for the night. I was in plenty of time to appear at the Passenger Terminal at 1000 hours the next morning, complete with luggage.

I found out much later that my 23-year younger brother, Lillis, had come through Travis on July 9, returning from his year in Viet Nam with the 101st Airborne.

Flight H243, a contract flight with Continental Airlines, a Boeing 707, took off on time, and my one year out of country began. We arrived in Honolulu well before sunset. We were there an hour to refuel and get serviced, and got off to stretch our legs. I had been at Honolulu once before, when our crew landed at Hickam AFB on our way to Guam in our RB-36, in 1955.

Off we went again, racing the sun, but it won, and set ahead of us. We were served two or three frozen TV dinners, heated, of course, but every time the cabin crew woke us up to eat, just about every other passenger lit up a cigarette. I nearly suffocated on their smoke.

Some time during the night, we crossed the International Date Line, so when we landed at Clark it was already July 12, not yet daylight. I reset my watch, got a ride over to the VOQ, checked in, drew all the blinds tight, and crashed on the bed for some much needed rest.

When I woke up, it was breakfast time. This was not my first time at Clark. In 1955 we had staged out of there on our way to do an RB-36 flyover of Bangkok, Thailand, celebrating some kind of holiday for them. That had been, so far as I knew, the only time that B-36's ever flew over the Continent of Asia. Clark seemed to have done a lot of building since my last visit eleven years earlier. And I didn't see any Jeepneys this time. Maybe they were just too decrepit to allow on Base.

Had I been superstitious, I'd have thought something funny was going on with me, related to the number 1--at the Travis VOQ, I had room 101. On Flight H243 I was No. 1 on the passenger list and was given boarding Pass No. 1, to occupy seat C-1. At Clark VOQ I was given Room No. 1, at the Survival School I was assigned Bed No. 1 in Tent 7. Was all that lucky or unlucky?

23

Rain on our arrival at Clark on Tuesday morning turned to hot, humid and sunny. I called Transportation, and got scheduled to fly on to Ton Son Nhut, at Saigon, check in time 0400 on Tuesday, the 19th. I spent Tuesday and Wednesday night in the VOQ, then moved to the Survival School tent on Wednesday. It was like the sixteen foot square tent covered hut I lived in while in Basic Training at Jefferson Barracks in 1943, just warmer. Some things don't change much over the years. Thursday was ground school, mainly a briefing on what we'd be doing out in the jungle for three days and nights. We were briefed also not to shave and risk infected cuts for the duration of the expedition.

Friday morning we were lifted by H-19 helicopters out to the training area, where we were joined by our instructor and his two Negrito assistants. The Negritos were barefooted, but what magnificent feet! They were wide, with straight, muscular toes and thick, muscular soles. The men were wiry little fellows, about four feet ten inches tall.

Each of us was carrying a pack including a blanket, a poncho, parachute cloth, mosquito net, insect repellant, a machete, two canteens with pouches, a canteen cup, a hunting knife, and other goodies. We left the grassy helicopter landing area, which was surrounded by pointed hills, and followed a logging road and then a rapidly running stream up to our camping area. I even walked across the stream on a log without falling off into the water. As we went along, the instructor identified various edible food plants, and showed us water trees. One makes a diamond shape cut in a water tree's bark, fits it with a bamboo stem, then collects the water that flows out of the cut, up to several gallons in a night. The water is pure, with a slight fruity taste. It did not have to be boiled or treated with iodine like the river water. The tree leaves collect moisture during the night and send the water down to the roots. The sap rises up in the tree in the daytime, supplying nutrients to the leaves.

We camped on a small island between two branches of the stream. Each of us used strategically spaced small saplings, strung a parachute cloth hammock among them, and made a roof of his waterproof poncho. We placed our mosquito nets under the ponchos and around the hammocks. Our gear was placed under the poncho to keep it dry.

To eat, we had C-rations, monkey bananas, rice (which we'd brought along), banana blossom, (boiled, then roasted), aggie palm hearts, and other jungle goodies.

The most useful plant is the banana, its big leaves are good for all kinds of things. Bamboo was also useful, one can use a section of a large stem to cook in. Monkey bananas are about three to four inches long, and delicious, but each one has at least a hundred seeds about the size of small grape seeds. One is kept busy spitting seeds while eating them.

The Negrito boys and some of their elders from the nearby village came to visit us. The boys were trying to learn to count in English, and one traced out his name in the dirt. One little boy eight or ten years old showed us how to make a bow and arrow with which he could shoot small birds, from the materials at hand. They lived nearby, and were dressed in rags, their Sunday Best, I assumed. From what the American instructor said, they probably wore nothing at home, and even the adults wore only loin cloths. Our Negrito instructors wore ragged pieces of fatigue uniforms.

Their staple food was rice, but they also raised corn, sugar cane, bananas and some of the foods we found in the jungle. Whenever they were leaving the village for several hours, they took their cooking pots along.

During World War II, the Negritos gave the Japanese a very hard time, even stealing into their barracks at night to behead some of them. They were said to have successfully hidden seven US pilots in the Clark Field area for three years.

The Negritos and the majority Filipinos of Asian extraction apparently did not get along too well, and the Philippine Government didn't do anything for the Negritos. The US Air Force hired many of the Negritos in various jobs around Clark, especially as guards, as well as instructors for the Survival School. Because of their help during World War II, the whole tribe was provided medical care by the US at the Clark Field Hospital.

Some of our guys bought bows and arrows from them.

The arrow tips were steel, very sharp. One elderly man, demonstrating his wares, shooting at an empty C-ration box fifty feet away, was more accurate than I would have been with a pistol.

Across the valley from where we camped was a tree harvest going on, cutting down big trees and converting them to logs to sell. Our guess was that they were going to Denmark to be made into dining room furniture and chairs.

On Sunday morning we broke camp and returned to the helicopter pad, where we each had a turn at being lifted into the chopper in a jungle penetrator sling.

About 3:00 p. m., we left our larger packs, took compass, medical kit, bug repellant, poncho, canteen, and parachute cloth with us, and got on a Six by Six. Each of us also was issued a small numbered metal tag.

We were hauled up a very rough road, then dropped off in twos and threes. The objective was to either walk in to a check-in point, or to get set for a helicopter pick up, between 0500 and 0600 the next morning. We were to avoid getting caught by any of the six designated Negrito trackers, with those magnificent feet, who would be starting out about 15 or 20 minutes behind us. I kind of thought each of the six had several lookers helping him. Any of us who was caught was to surrender the small numbered metal tag that had been issued to him. A successful tracker could then turn in the tag to the survival school for a three pound sack of rice.

Two airmen and I got off the truck at the base of a very steep hill, and climbed up it, hanging on to bushes along the way. At the top, we found ourselves on a very small peak, but we were able to follow a quite narrow ridge, without falling off on either side of it, to a bigger hill. We just had time to make our way to the end of this new ridge, from which there was no way down, when we saw a Negrito coming. We got down as low as we could in the tall grass on the three foot wide ridge, and saw some other fellows get caught.

Finally, after waiting for a very long time, we climbed up to where we could see. We saw a likely knob from which the helicopter could pick us up the next morning, and made our way to it. We concluded it would be o. k., then made our way back to a grove of banana trees to spend the night. We made banana leaf beds, and banana leaf shelters to keep off any rain, just as it was getting dark. Dark comes down quite suddenly in that part of the world. We had just gotten settled in when a Negrito came walking by, but he didn't see us in the dark grove.

It didn't rain. I had thoroughly smeared all my exposed skin areas with mosquito repellent, and though hundreds of the critters buzzed around my ears all night, I did get some sleep, and didn't get a single bite. Some time after midnight, Sgt. Mulligan said,

" Whatever you are, you can have my bed!", and got up.

Something had crawled through his hair. It was probably a gecko (lizard) looking for mosquitos.

When morning came, we packed up and made our way to our selected pick up point, laid out our parachute panels as a signal, and waited for our pick up. The hilltop was smaller in diameter than the H-19's main rotor, but they hovered and dropped their sling down to pick us up one at a time. It was lots easier getting off that hill than getting on it had been. After everyone had been picked up, they flew us back to base, six at a time.

After a shave and a shower, and clean clothes, I looked, felt, and smelled, a lot better. The bed felt good, too.

It had been quite an adventure, and I felt that I could survive if ever I were shot down, or crash landed, in the jungle.

The next morning I was once more over the ocean, in an old but comfortable DC-6. The stewardesses brought us hot wash cloths to freshen up with, then served us a delicious hot lunch. Our last luxury for a while!

Figure 3.1
　　The National Flag of the Republic of Viet Nam

CHAPTER III

WELL, HERE I AM

Suddenly I found myself at the busiest airport I had ever seen. There were many kinds of aircraft, from O-1's to big jets, and lots of helicopters. No wonder the airfield was such a tempting mortar target for the Viet Cong.

The airport terminal was as near bedlam as I had ever seen. Apparently people of all conditions traveled by air. Some pieces of baggage I saw looked like sacks of walnuts, or something similar.

The bus ride to Quarters was dusty, but rain came later.

I was assigned temporary lodging in new raw wood quarters. We were told that if a mortar attack came, we should run for the latrine--it was built of concrete.

While I was en route, the 6250th Combat Support Group had become the 377th Combat Support Group. They probably hadn't even changed phone numbers.

During the day I happened to walk past the post office, so I checked to see if there were any mail for me. Much to my surprise, there was a letter from Alberta's sister, Anna Mary. It had taken less than five days to come from the Kansas City area. That was quicker than people were making it.

I met my erstwhile B-52 Aircraft Commander, John R. McCormick, for a three hour dinner and visit at the small Officers' Club. I had taken command of his crew when he left Ellsworth AFB. The next familiar face I saw in the Club was Bob Kaiser, who took over the crew when I left Sheppard AFB to attend AFIT. He was now flying C-123's. Mac told me of other men we had both known over the years who were now in theater. What a small world! Mac was working in the Operations Section of Seventh Air Force. Everybody was getting his turn in SEA.

Mac gave me a ride from the Club to my quarters on his Honda scooter, and dodging chuckholes full of water was quite a series of maneuvers.

There was a curfew from midnight to 0430, no Americans

Figure 3.2
Ton Son Nhut, the World's Busiest Airport

and presumably no Vietnamese were allowed on the streets during those hours. Mac lived about four miles from the airport. He said it was about another mile to downtown.

I could hear airplanes running up, taxiing and taking off all night long. In the background was the boom-boom of artillery fire. I thought, optimistically, that it was our side bombarding theirs. And there was heavy rain. My room mate for the night was Capt. R. M. Howell. He was on the way home, his year complete. His Commander at Phan Rang had been Col. Pensinger, whom I knew. Howell had a house and family just East of Wichita, in an area I knew. What a small world.

Next morning I was moved to the Martin Hotel, Annex #2, at 241 Bis. Le Van Duyet, right in the middle of Saigon. Le Van Duyet was one of the " main drags" of town, not far from one of the main Pagodas.

I was scheduled to leave on Saturday, the 14th, for Pleiku. My station was to be at Qui Nhon, as ALO (Air Liaison Officer) with the 22nd Division of ARVN (Army of the Republic of Viet Nam). The folks who made the decision worked at the same place Mac did. I spent most of the day finding out what the job was supposed to be. Mac scheduled himself to come by and pick me up for dinner, but when he got to my place the Vietnamese guard wouldn't let him in. So I missed dinner. I should have been out front to see him coming.

It was like old home week. While processing in I encountered other old friends and acquaintances, among them Bill Rottler from my AFIT class. He was on his way to Bien Hoa to fly F-100's, and said another classmate, Bob Artz, was in the pipeline for the same assignment. I asked the Catholic Chaplain if he knew Father Sullivan, whose going away party we had attended only a short time before at Wright-Patterson. He said he did, and Father Sullivan had been assigned to Pleiku. I was told I'd be TDY at Pleiku for several days before going on to Qui Nhon, for briefings and in-country check out in the O-1.

I got a huge gamma globulin shot, to protect me against hepatitis. It probably would not protect me from any of the other bugs going around. I also took my first anti-malarial pill. I'd be taking that one every Thursday.

Mac and I did get together on Thursday evening. We went out to eat at the Rex Hotel, down town. The Rex bar and dining room were on the top floor, about the seventh story. There was a good view across town. Straight across the street from the Rex was the Street of Flowers, so called because it was a gorgeous flower market, with many stalls. It must have been the gladiolus season, there were lots of them.

At the other end of the Street of Flowers was the Saigon River, where the ships came in to unload. We rode down to the river, and then along it, seeing, among other things, the floating restaurant that had been blown up a year or so earlier. It had been repaired, and was doing big business.

The main shopping area was right around the Rex. The shop windows were filled with nice merchandise. On the sidewalks around them were many street vendors. Much of their goods looked like it had come from BX's. It was probably stolen from the ships, or the docks or warehouses along the river. Mac took me for a ride around town, showing me many of the more famous buildings, such as government headquarters, Presidential Palace, city hall and so on.

Traffic in town was unbelievable. There were horse drawn carts, bicycles, three wheel cycles with passenger in front, same arrangement with a motor, three wheeled scooters with driver in front and six seats in back, Renault taxis, small cars, big cars, French cars, German cars, British cars, Japanese cars, and trucks of every description. Mac said there was no speed limit, and gasoline was plentiful. Speed was limited by rough streets and congestion. There were some traffic lights, and policemen directing traffic at many of the busier intersections.

CHAPTER IV

LEARNING THE ROPES

Early on Saturday morning, Day 14 (July 23), I was on my way again, in a C-130, to Pleiku. It was at the West end of Route 19, not very far from Laos and Cambodia. The East end of Route 19 was at the harbor at Qui Nhon.

The C-130 was a real work horse for transporting supplies and people " in country". C-47's, C-123's and Army Caribous played a similar role.

Pleiku's most conspicuous airplanes were A-1E's and A-1H's. Most numerous were UH-1 helicopters (Hueys). The Army seemed to regard them the same as Jeeps, just used for longer runs than Jeeps. Aircraft, including O-1's, were parked in sand bag protected revetments, to at least partly shelter them from mortar attacks.

Headquarters for the Second Corps (II Corps) Military Operations Area were in Pleiku. That included various Vietnamese Commanders and staffs, and Senior American Advisors and their staffs.

I picked up some more processing, and drew some more equipment, including a new watch, a survival vest containing survival radio, tropical first aid kit and other goodies, a big, white Pilot's crash helmet with visor, mike and earphones, a .38 caliber pistol and an M-16, with ammunition. I had no plans to fire them.

I also met some of the people at Pleiku with whom and for whom I'd be working. One of them was Lt. Col. Orville O. Scroggin. He was the II (Two) Corps ALO, and my new immediate boss. I was scheduled to fly about six times for my in-country check-out. The present ALO at the 22nd ARVN was Major Max Pettijohn, scheduled to return Stateside in February 1967. Where he would go upon my arrival no one said.

Still continuing the small world thing, sure enough the newly assigned Catholic Chaplain was Father (Captain) Sullivan, who had left Wright-Patterson not far ahead of me. The senior Catholic Chaplain was Father (Lt. Col.) Sullivan, US Army.

The basic Viet Nam money unit was the dong (Vietnamese), or piastre (French), or "P" (American). 118 of them equalled the US dollar. Americans were allowed to exchange them only at US finance offices or other US facilities, such as Officers' Clubs. Americans were not authorized to give US dollars to any Vietnamese.

Pleiku was an old French military town and base. It was there that some 30 US Marines had made the news by being killed in a Viet Cong attack on their barracks one night a year or so earlier.

The base was expanding and being built up rapidly. There was a good runway and a small Army Hospital, in rounded metal buildings a lot like the Nissen huts I lived in, in England, in 1944. The US 25th Infantry was encamped nearby. The Army people and the hospital staff lived in tents, surrounded by a sea of mud. I'd bet some of the tents leaked, too.

I was blessed to stay in a wooden barracks. There was no glass in the windows, only screens and louvered closures on the outside. That kept the rain out, but not the wind. The temperature must have been in the lower 60's, I was wearing my jacket to keep warm. In July, not far from the Equator?

What it was, of course, was the Summer (Southwest) Monsoon. Pleiku was in the Highlands, about 2500 feet above sea level. Warm, moist air from the Southwest, coming from over the Indian Ocean across the Gulf of Siam, was cooled as it came over the rising terrain, and formed low, wet clouds, dropping lots of its moisture as rain in the process. Result? Cool, soupy weather.

I turned a whole sack full of dirty laundry over to the maid: 20 P for a fatigue uniform, less for underwear and socks.

My once hoped for airplane--a C-141--came in every day, bringing in fresh troops and picking up others to return to the US.

I got a little inkling about one aspect of my upcoming job. The Army Brigadier General who commanded the support forces in the Qui Nhon area called to ask that the man I was to replace be removed immediately. When told that I would be there shortly, he agreed to leaving the man there until I arrived.

It appeared that my first job upon arrival in Qui Nhon would be to get the Air Force back in the good graces of the Army. That was vital because the Air Force depended on the Army for support. Perhaps all my years in SAC and ASD would help.

I started getting a series of briefings on my new job, but then there was another call from Qui Nhon about the friction between the Army BG and the Air Force Major. It was decided that Scroggin and I would fly down to Qui Nhon for the day to see if we could placate the General. A C-47 was scheduled to go right after noon. We put on clean uniforms and ate lunch. We went to Operations, the pilot filed a flight plan, and we cranked up to go. But, on run up, the left propeller wouldn't feather. The feathering motor had to be replaced, and there wasn't a new one on base. We tried to bum a ride on an airplane going through, but all the seats were full.

By then, the weather had improved, so we decided to go in an O-1. We started up and taxied out, and the radio went dead. We returned to the flight line, and the mechanics found the starter switch had stuck. They changed the switch and the voltage regulator, but then the starter wouldn't work. It had burned out because, with the stuck switch, it turned with the engine. They started to change the starter, then found there wasn't a replacement available on base. By then it was five o'clock, so we gave up for the day.

Scroggin lived in the MACV (Military Assistance Command Vietnam) compound, and invited me to have dinner with him at their club. There was a separate nice dining room for Lt. Cols. and above, and they all ate together every night. The senior officer was Col. Lee, US Army. He seemed like a fine man, and all the other men obviously liked and respected him.

Figure 5.1
 Qui Nhon from the West

Figure 5.2
 Route 19 Leading to Qui Nhon Harbor

CHAPTER V

QUI NHON - TEMPORARILY

The next morning (Day 17), Scroggin and I flew an O-1 down to Qui Nhon, with toilet kits and changes of clothes in brief cases, prepared to stay over night. That turned into several days. Same old Air Force routine--clothes, and laundry out, were at one place, duty was at another. Getting a head start on the laundry problem in Qui Nhon, I sent a set of fatigues, a set of underwear and a pair of socks home with the maid on Friday morning; she brought them back the next morning, nicely done up.

On Saturday a letter from home came for me, my first. The news was only four days old! Everybody was fine.

I met some of the personnel with whom I'd be working. The Army's 22nd Advisory Group were all very fine people, completely sold on the work being done by the FAC's and the ALO. My concern about not getting much flying time went away. My predecessor, Major Max Pettijohn, had been getting seventy hours per month. When we arrived he had gone to Kontum to check in with his new boss there. He'd be working for my Hurlburt classmate, Lt. Col. Charles V. Gibson.

The ALO and the FAC's were not supposed to fly more than 85 hours per month, could get a waiver to fly up to 100, and if absolutely necessary could go up to 120. More than that was absolutely forbidden. What it boiled down to was a shortage of pilots.

I rode in the back seat with Capt. Bill Richards, one of the FAC's I was inheriting, in an O-1, on a regular FAC mission. I got a look at part of Binh Dinh Province, the primary operational area for the FAC's at Qui Nhon. It was a mixture of mountains, rice paddies, regular farming, and little hamlets or villages. The rice growing area was low lying and flat, with water standing in most of the paddies. It extended from the irregular coast line to the next range of hills thirty miles or so West, with a quite irregular border. Another range of hills, called the Phu Cats, ran East and West some distance to the North.

Between Qui Nhon and the Phu Cats was a wide valley plain, with a substantial stream flowing West to East across it. There were numerous small hamlets, connected by narrow roads that flooded widely in the rainy season. Normally the hamlets showed lots of human activity, but the Northern part of the area had been turned over to the ROK Capital Division for rounding up the Viet Cong. Their way was to move the farm folks out, then those still there were the Viet Cong, more easily dealt with. The hamlets so affected and the paddies around them had grown up in weeds, and were easily identified from the air. Many of the evacuees had ended up as refugees in Qui Nhon.

In places the scenery was quite beautiful. The airport was West across town from the harbor, with a range of hills behind it.

It appeared that the enthusiasm of the people we supported, for the way we, the FAC's and the ALO, did our jobs, was going to help make my task easier.

I also met Dai-ta (Col.) Nguyen-Van-Hieu, Commander of the 22nd ARVN. He spoke English quite well, and impressed me very favorably.

The 22nd's military area of responsibility covered three provinces, Binh Dinh, Phu Yen and Phu Bon. So, as the 22nd's new ALO, I was also picking up responsibility for FAC operations out of Tuy Hoa (Province Phu Yen), and out of Cheo Reo (Phu Bon). Tuy Hoa was South along the coast, while Cheo Reo was Southwest of Qui Nhon across a lot of jungle territory and rough terrain.

The quarters for us and the Army Advisors were in the old French military barracks in town, sort of mid way between the harbor and the airport. A portion of the second floor was assigned to Army nurses who worked in the local Army Hospital. The rest of the complex, besides quarters, provided for the Army Officers' Mess, the Club Area, a small second floor auditorium, and various administrative offices.

The FAC's and the ALO were assigned two rooms on the ground floor, with a connecting bath, four beds (two double deck bunks) in each room. The ALO's front door was only two doors

Figure 5.4
ALO/FAC Office and Quarters

Figure 5.3
Old French Military Quarters in Qui Nhon

away from the Mail Room. With only three people assigned, there was room for house guests. There were plenty of them. Pettijohn was gone, and no one slept in his bed, but six beds were filled that first night. We hosted two young Army Officers, and an Air Force Major. The weather that first day was hot and humid with showers, not unlike Fairborn in July. It certainly was different from the cool, wet weather at Pleiku, only 85 or 90 miles West, on the plateau.

The ALO/FAC Radio room was in a small building only a few steps from the main building. Just beyond that was the Port Commanding General's combination Quarters and Operations building.

There was no Electrical Power Utility company, so each building had its own generating system. The brightness of the lights depended on how many lights and fans were operating.

The hassle with the Army Support Group's CG turned out to be because of his dissatisfaction with the appearance and military courtesy of the Air Force people in the area. General Meyer didn't think Major Pettijohn, as the senior Air Force Officer, had been doing enough to keep the Air Force troops in line. A Major did not come out too well in discussions with an Army General.

Keeping him satisfied could turn out to be a ticklish job. The situation had the potential of testing my political skills. The General had no voice in our operations, but he was charged with maintaining military courtesy and discipline by all US military members in the area. So he had his problems, too.

It was apparent that I'd get used to seeing little bare bottoms. Most of the little tots under about four years old did not wear any pants. It looked like a minor sanitation problem to me, but since they may not have gotten bathed very often, perhaps it was better than trying to keep them in diapers. Our maid had a little son, Tanh, about four years old, who came to work with her. He wore a little sport shirt and shorts. He was a happy little guy, who liked to salute.

The ALO/FAC Section, Officers and Airmen, had a beer party and hamburger broil down at the flight line on Friday night.

It was a good visiting and talking kind of party, and everybody seemed to have a good time. Beers available were Ba-muoi-Ba (Thirty-Three) (Vietnamese) and San Miguel (Filipino). But there was a curfew for military personnel from 2200 to 0600, so we all had to be back at quarters by 10:00 p. m.

I had a long and interesting conversation with a Vietnamese soldier, rank about equivalent to a US Corporal. He was an interpreter between US and VN Army and Air Force people. He was twenty-three, had been married a year and a half, and was about to become a father. His mother, father and twenty-two year old sister lived in Saigon. His father, if I understood correctly, had been out of his mind (crazy, he said) since 1954. His twenty-five year old brother was in the Army, his twenty year old brother worked for a contractor in Cam Ranh. His sister wanted to join the VN Army, he said to be a WAC, but it sounded like she'd be a combination nurse and social worker.

His name was Phuoc (probably his family name). He had had seven years of school, including six or eight months of English.

Phuoc was seriously concerned with the future of his country, and the leadership. Some of his observations:

Vietnamese did not dare criticize the government for fear of being punished. (I didn't think that was completely true, at least not at the civilian level; Vietnamese newspapers in English frequently criticized the central government.)

General Ky was too young to lead the country. An old man would be much wiser and know better how to lead the people. However, he did not know of any such present leader in Viet Nam. To be wise, one had to be old.

Vietnamese people were handicapped because they did not know how to do things with machines, only with their hands.

It would have been a good idea to drop an Atom Bomb on Hanoi. That would kill only one million people. If the war were to go on for ten years, we would kill two million people.

One way to win the war would be to invade North Viet Nam.

Some of his observations about American GI's:

GI's were very kind to children, always being nice to them, giving them candy and so on.

GI's were careful drivers. They stopped at Stop signs and looked in all directions before going. Korean and Vietnamese drivers did not stop, and did not look.

GI's did not bargain. They paid the first price asked, so there were two prices on everything, American price and Vietnamese price. This made the prices of everything go up. Rice used to sell for 8 P per kilo, now it sold for 25 P. GI's should bargain so prices would not go up.

Other views:

President Diem, who had been assassinated three years earlier, was a good leader, but his brother Ngo Dinh Nhu and his sister-in-law, Madame Nhu, were a bad influence on him.

I thought Phuoc was quite astute for a man his age.

Our maid was called Mama-san, like all maids for GI's in the Far East. She was about four feet ten inches tall, and weighed less than 90 pounds. She swept, dusted, made the beds, cleaned the bathroom, brought hot coffee and drinking water. For all this the Billeting Office paid her. When she took laundry home to do, we paid her. She charged me 40 P for a fatigue uniform, a pair of heavy socks and a set of underwear, overnight service. That was the equivalent of about 35 or 40 cents American.

The left side of Mama-san's face and her left hand were very badly scarred. I didn't speak Vietnamese and she didn't speak American, but one of the guys who did speak her language told me that she and her mother lived in Hanoi in 1954 when the Communists took over. Mama-san must have been about 15 at the time. They arrested her and her mother, most likely because they were Catholics. They didn't mess much with her mother, they simply cut her head off. They poured gasoline on this then young daughter, and set her on fire, hence all the scars. She must have come South with some of the refugees that Dr. Tom Dooley helped. Mama-san's husband was in the VN Army, at Pleiku. Little Tanh played with his toy airplane while his Mama did the cleaning. Mama-san wore an Our Lady of Lourdes Medal, confirming that she was Catholic.

Figure 5.6
Mama-san and Tanh

My Year in Viet Nam

There was a "Hail and Farewell" party for Advisory Group 22. Of the ALO/FAC's, Maj. Max Pettijohn was leaving for Kontum (North of Pleiku); Capt. Dallas Coffield was rotating back to the States; Maj. Bill Coon was arriving from Pleiku, and Lt. Col. John Welch was scheduled to arrive just any day.

I found it interesting that a highway and a railroad ran parallel to each other all the way between Hanoi and Saigon. Over most of the distance, however, there had been no train nor motor vehicle traffic for quite some time. The VC had continuously ambushed train and road traffic, had blown up the road beds and torn up the rails. Until the bombing in the North, the roads and rails there had been in good shape. Now they, too, were not usable on a dependable basis. It looked like a tremendous challenge to rebuild them once the war was over.

After a week at Qui Nhon filled with learning experiences, I got back up to Pleiku, with heavy rain, and nicely done up laundry waiting for me. The maid must have wondered if I were ever coming back.

I needed about three days of flyable weather to finish my in-country check out.

The log jam in the mail department broke loose the next morning. I received seven letters that had been forwarded from Saigon.

Flying broke loose, too. I got 3:15 flying time in the afternoon, practicing landings and navigation, and trying to see things under the trees. I also fired a couple of target marking rockets. There was a laterite (mixed clay and gravel) runway used by the 4th Infantry, next to a Special Forces Camp, on which we got a couple of landings, piece of cake. I found myself soaking wet from perspiration when we made our final landing for the day. I was credited with two missions, leaving only four to go.

On day 27, the Instructor Pilot and I visited two Special Forces (Green Berets) camps. They were modern day primitive forts, armed with hand weapons and some bigger guns. They were dug in, protected by sandbags and barbed wire. These two were manned by small teams of American soldiers, less than ten, who commanded hundreds of Montagnards, Vietnamese hill people. The Montagnards had their village right next to or inside the camp, with their families. They were paid and provided with food and medical care by the Americans. Each camp had an air strip where an airplane as big as a C-123 could land--no problem for an O-1.

These camps sent out patrols who looked for the Viet Cong, harassed them and tried to keep track of where they were. In turn they were sometimes attacked by the VC or by the North Vietnamese Army (NVA). When that happened they would call for help, and their FAC would call in fighter bombers to drive off and destroy the attacking force. The Free World and ARVN forces would also send in ground support. About then the attack would stop and the VC would fade away to become conspirators in the jungle, and perhaps farmers in the fields and rice paddies, until they thought the time was ripe for another attack.

Those who suffered the most were the women, children and old men of the villages friendly to our side, especially next to the Special Forces camps. They sometimes suffered heavy casualties, killed and injured, in an attack. One US Army man in one of the camps we visited said they had been attacked early in July. If I remembered correctly, twenty some women and children were killed outright, and more than seventy were injured, some with arms and legs blown off, and so on. I thought that kind of action got American service men's hearts really into this war.

Most pilots who flew around Pleiku were familiar with a mountain a few miles South of town, universally known in pilot slang as P____ Mountain, because of its apearance, resembling a part of female anatomy. Aircraft flying low in bad weather, following primitive roads, sometimes crashed into it, and their wreckage could be seen on its slopes.

At Sunday Mass on Day 28, Father Sullivan made a plea for the St. Paul Orphanage in Pleiku. The collection was for it. Two Catholic Sisters from the Orphanage attended the Mass, and passed the collection plates. Father gave an inspirational talk, stressing the Orphanage's needs, and the advantages of giving. He said money is like manure, it's no good unless you spread it

My Year in Viet Nam

Figure 5.6
    Pleiku, Town and Base Area

Figure 5.7
    P____ Mountain

around. Then he quoted a line from The Sound of Music:

"A bell is not a bell until you ring it, a song is not a song until you sing it, love is not love until you give it."

That was when I decided to put in ten dollars.

Father said the average total collection at three Sunday Masses had been $98. At this Mass alone it was $475. Americans are a generous lot.

Father gave me a copy of the Wright-Patter, the Wright-Patterson weekly paper. I looked for names I knew and any jokes. I gave it to Ed Hammer, who had also been at Wright-Patterson. He began reading the new regulations on parking on the base, windshield stickers, etc. At first he chuckled, then laughed, and by the time he got to the end he was darn near hysterical. The rules were so complicated they were ridiculous. If one parked at the Hospital, Chapel, Commissary or the Base Exchange, he'd be all right. If he parked anywhere else the whole base police organization would collapse.

I flew 3:40 that Sunday, and directed fighter strikes on three target areas. Each had small pole and thatch buildings, which were suspected of being used by the VC for storage, over night rest stops, or what have you. That left me with one more flight to complete my in-country check out

I did indeed get that flight on August 8, Day 30.

We dropped in at Kontum, which was the working headquarters of the 24th Special Zone. We paid a brief visit to the Catholic Orphanage. They had lots of orphans, and needed lots of help.

We spent most of the time just looking at the ground in an area about the size of a Kansas county, just to see what we could see. For the last half hour or so, we were helping look for an eleven vehicle convoy which had supposedly started up the highway North toward Kontum, but disappeared. Since the highway North of Pleiku had no paved turnoffs before Kontum, we couldn't understand where they could have gone. Finally we got a call on the radio saying they'd been found. Trying to be funny, we asked,

"Where? In the motor pool?"

The answer was,

"Well, something like that."

So we really didn't know whether they never started out, or just got scared and came back.

The next day I got everything completed at Pleiku, and returned to Qui Nhon.

CHAPTER VI

QUI NHON FOR REAL

Wednesday, August 10, Day 32, there was lots of mail waiting in Qui Nhon for me. The latest letter had taken only three days to come, from Columbia, Missouri, where the family stopped on the way to a vacation in Kansas at Alberta's Mother's farm, where Alberta grew up.

We had neighbors in Fairborn, to whom I wrote, Marie and Bob Behr, and Suzie and Bernie Borden. Marie was from Belgium, and Suzie was from Paris, native French speakers. Bob had grown up in Berlin. Bernie was from a Jewish community in New York. I invited the ladies to write to me in French, which I had studied in school, and Bob to write to me in German, which I had also studied in school. I told Bernie to write to me in anything but Yiddish.

It was a surprise to me to learn the privileges that went with being a Lt. Col. I started off by being assigned the better of the two FAC/ALO rooms all by myself, though I still had the two double deck bunk beds. There was some talk I might get a room on the second floor, which might have been cooler. But the one where I was, was most convenient, close to the mail room, a one minute walk to the dining hall, less than 50 feet to our radio room. That was important, the radio room was our nerve center. Potable water was available at a spigot on the outside rear of the dining hall.

The room was about 12 X 15 feet, with a tile floor. The shared bath was standard, lavatory, toilet, shower. A rather dilapidated curtain kept some of the water in the area of the shower.

The front door opened off a long sheltered sort of porch, formed by the overhang of the outside walk of the second floor. Opposite the door, inside, was a large screened window. There was a screened window all across the wall above the door. A slow turning fan, like those of stores before air conditioning, was mounted in the ceiling. Electrical power was fifty cycle, 220

Fiure 6.1
   Jeep Row

Figure 6.2
   Port Commander's Offices and Quarters

volts. American appliances would work with a transformer. Light bulbs had a bayonet base instead of a screw in base. A closet in one corner was heated full time by a light bulb, to keep clothes dry and decrease mildew problems.

The beds were standard Army steel bunks with foam rubber mattresses, covered by sheets. They were firm, but hot to sleep on. The pillows smelled. There was a mosquito netting all the way around one lower bunk, so I chose that one.

I heard a dog fight just outside the door. The dogs were fighting in the same language they used in Kansas.

A Ford built swing axle Jeep was assigned to me. I parked it at the end of the building, with all the others assigned to the Advisors. It was about a fourteen mile drive to Division Headquarters at Ba Gi, and I expected to make the drive several times a week. The streets in town were quite rough, and the road to the base wasn't much better. 15 mph was about all that could be tolerated in town, and I seldom got up to 40 on the highway.

Sort of inadvertently, I made a surprising and alarming discovery, Army nurses had been going along in the back seat on some FAC missions. I stopped that immediately! I didn't see how I could possibly write a letter to a mother explaining that her nurse daughter had been shot down on a combat mission.

Another new rule that I put into effect--except in an emergency or to stay under a low ceiling, we would fly no lower than 1500 feet above the ground. At that altitude, the likelihood of being hit by small arms fire from the ground was minimal. Also, we could see areas and activities on the ground that we'd miss if we were lower.

Our FAC Radio call sign was Herb. So, in my position as leading FAC with the 22nd ARVN, my call sign whenever I was in an O-1 became Herb 01 (Herb Zero One).

I learned that to the Vietnamese, Number One is the very best, Number Ten is the very worst. So, was I the best?

I flew a FAC mission on Friday, and on Saturday morning drove out to Ba Gi, to attend the staff meeting with US Army Col. Hunter, Senior American Advisor to the Division. That was interesting and informative.

My Year in Viet Nam

Figure 6.3
First Cavalry's Shoulder Patch, on the Hill Above their Base at An Khe

Figue 6.4
Barbed Wire Barriers Around An Khe

My Year in Viet Nam

Rumors should be discounted, but it was rumored that General Meyer, who was upset at the state of discipline and military courtesy among the Air Force contingent, would soon retire. He had been often seen but little heard from in recent days.

I had been borrowing another FAC's maps when going flying, but spent a good part of the day, after return from Ba Gi on Saturday, making up clear plastic covered maps for my own use in flying over my assigned area. The plastic cover protected the maps from wear, and made it possible to mark items, like targets, with grease pencil, and then wipe the marks off. They were on a scale of 50,000 to one--one inch on the map equaled 50,000 inches on the ground. Do the math, 50,000 inches equal .789 mile. Actually the maps were scaled in the Army's Military Grid metric system, with each small block on the map equal to a kilometer. It was thus possible to plot a fix quite accurately. A map of Kansas to that scale would be about 20 X 40 feet. So for a longer trip or larger area, it took several maps, which we had to somehow fit into the cockpit.

The routine was falling into place. I flew 1630 to 1900 on Saturday evening, and flew again at 1300 on Sunday.

One of my radio operators, Sgt. Smith, hadn't been paid since leaving his family on July 11, so I took him along on a trip to Pleiku on Monday. On the way, we ran into the Plateau bad weather, so we turned back and landed at An Khe, the First Cavalry Base. You'd know it was their hangout because they had a large color picture of their shoulder patch painted high on the hill West of their field. Interesting note: there were multiple barbed wire barriers around the base.

We had lunch, and I visited with one of the First Cav's FAC's. The weather improved a bit, so we flew on to Pleiku, where I ran my errands while Sgt. Smith got his pay problem straightened out, and was paid.

I was getting a bit more settled in. I flew to visit Tuy Hoa, about 50 miles South down the coast, and to Cheo Reo, across miles of jungle South and West of Qui Nhon. Tuy Hoa's general airport sat between a mountain and the town South of it, and had a PSP (Pierced Steel Planking) runway. The FAC's flew out of there. That runway often had fine dust on it. When there had been a shower, it was like landing on a greased surface. South of Tuy Hoa, across a lazy looking river, was a large sandy beach area, on which a fighter base was built.

Cheo Reo was getting a new, wider runway, blacktop.

Both towns were operating sites for some of my FAC's. I ordinarily did not supervise them, but was held responsible to a certain degree for their operations. They were given targets and flew VR (Visual Reconnaissance) on their own, and supported friendly forces in their areas. The FAC's filling those jobs were enthusiastic and doing well.

Most of the area between Tuy Hoa and Cheo Reo appeared to be uninhabited. Such also was the case between Cheo Reo and the Province border to the West. Along some of the trails were areas of deciduous trees that looked like autumn had come; the leaves had turned color and were falling off. This was where the Ranch Hands (C-123's and their crews) had sprayed Agent Orange. The objective was to remove the cover from which the Viet Cong could set up ambushes. The trees were not killed; after a time the foliage grew back.

One of my airmen must have thought my Jeep looked cruddy, he volunteered to wash it while I attended an Airfield Commander's Meeting. Actually, he took it to a Vietnamese car wash place, with a sign out front that said " Rua Xe" (Cars Washed). It had a gasoline powered pump drawing water out of a small irrigation ditch. Enterprising!

Even the entertainers were coming to Viet Nam. Arthur Godfrey was a guest of General Meyer, and I got a look at him, but did not get to talk to him.

With the westerly wind coming down off the plateau, the weather continued hot 24 hours a day.

Since a separate office was not available to me, I requested issue of a desk, an office chair, and a two drawer safe, to make my room also my office.

My activities began picking up. On Day 39, I took off on my first flight at 0700, and landed from my fourth one at 1900.

The first flight was VR, the last three were business trips to Pleiku, Cheo Reo and return, total flight time for the day, 4:20.

The next day, Friday, I spent most of the morning at Division Headquarters with the Division Staff and their US Army Advisors. It was a good thing the key Vietnamese Officers spoke English.

Directed fighter strikes were scheduled by Seventh Air Force, out of Saigon. Directing such a strike went like this: Our radio room would get a message directing us to put in a strike by a flight of fighters, usually jets, with bombs, and ammunition for strafing. The FAC selected for the mission would copy the encoded map coordinates of the target, apply the daily security additive (provided by 7th Air Force) to determine the exact target coordinates, copy the type of fighters and the fighter call sign, their radio frequency and time on target, the type of target; select the necessary maps, take off to get to the target ahead of the fighters.

Once in the target area, the FAC would fly straight across or near it to identify the aiming points and the best direction to attack, but without overtly displaying any interest in it.

Approaching the area, the fighters would check in on radio, tell the FAC their ordnance load, and be briefed by the FAC on the appearance of the target area and the direction of attack. We carried a standard aerial map with TACAN stations and radials, and distance circles plotted on it. We could then give the flight leader the radial and approximate distance from a TACAN. (One day an F-4 pilot landed at Qui Nhon and wanted to see the 0-1's TACAN receiver. We didn't have one.) Once the FAC and the fighter pilots had established visual contact with each other, the FAC would roll in on the target and fire a Willy Pete, then tell the fighters the clock direction and number of meters from the white smoke to the desired aiming point. He'd then clear them in "Hot", and stay out of the way.

The fighters would make their dive-bombing passes, and the FAC would give corrections from the bomb bursts for succeeding bombing passes. Strafing usually followed the bomb runs. The fighter flight leader would tell the FAC when all

My Year in Viet Nam

ordnance had been expended, and the FAC would fly over the target to assess the damage done. He'd give the fighters the Bomb Damage Assessment (BDA), thank them, and release them to return to base.

For dive bombing, I liked the A-1E's and A-1H's the best. They could loiter while a target was being sorted out, whereas the jets, F-100's and F-4's, were fuel limited, and couldn't hang around. Also, the A-1's dived at a lower speed and were more accurate. The best of all were A-1's flown by Vietnamese pilots. They had years of experience. One flight leader I directed made most of his passes inverted, rolling out just before bomb release.

On Friday afternoon I flew a combined strike mission and VR mission. I didn't enjoy the strike missions. The targets could be villages or other points that our Intelligence told us were being used by VC or NVA troops. Even though the buildings were built only of poles, mud and rice straw, I knew the personal effort that went into building things, so I couldn't take pleasure in destroying them. Even so, we did get big explosions of ordnance, reports of food stores destroyed and enemy killed, often enough to know we were being effective.

Some people seemed to enjoy the destruction, but not I. I prayed that no innocent people would be hurt, and that those who through their own destructive acts brought such loss and suffering to their own people would soon be convinced they couldn't win, and let peace come.

There was an area West of Qui Nhon that had once been farmed, but was now abandoned and barren. Out in the middle of it was a hut at coordinates which Saigon's Intelligence folks said were the source of enemy radio signals. They sent two F-4's, which, after several tries, hadn't hit the hut. Finally the wing man flew a pass just above the ground and dropped his bomb. It went through the hut and out the other side a hundred yards or more, and did not explode. The VC had another supply of land mine materials. I doubted the validity of the target to begin with.

I flew along about a 30 mile stretch of highway and railroad between Qui Nhon and Tuy Hoa. The Communists had destroyed every bridge, and had dug trenches half or all the way across the road in too many places to count.

Apparently the Communists believed that if they could destroy enough facilities and leaders, they could eventually move in to fill the vacuum. As much as I disliked--maybe hated was a better word--war, I hoped my part in it would help bring peace to that part of the world.

Sadly, my philosophy about war was tied in to my love of flying. Flying is a wonderful accomplishment of man, capable of doing tremendous good for mankind. Much of my flying had been connected either with destroying or in training in how to destroy. That was a prostitution of a marvelous art and skill. I was sad to have to so misuse it.

Visual Reconnaissance (VR) was basically just going out to see what we could see. Always we were looking for signs on the surface of what the enemy was doing. Sometimes we had special areas of interest, and would fly over an area to confirm an Intelligence report, sometimes we'd be looking for changes from the last time someone looked. With no special object in mind, we'd just be looking for indicators of human activities in areas where there were no friendlies. All items of interest, such as a previously unnoted foot trail, or the corner of a roof not seen before, were reported to the Intelligence Sections. One of my regular routes took me along Highway 1. It seemed that almost every morning there'd be new hand-dug trenches overlapping half way across it, or all the way across it. I thought perhaps that was how the VC got their daily (nightly) physical training.

Preplanned strike missions anywhere in the three province area had to be approved by the 22nd ARVN Commander, Col. Hieu. He knew, through his Intelligence Section, and innocent looking spies walking around, just where the VC were, where the friendly population and troops were, and so how to avoid injury to the people on our side.

When active fighting was going on, we either already had a FAC over the area, or as quickly as we could, got a FAC there. The FAC's job was to locate the "good guys" and the "bad guys" call for appropriate air support, direct the fighter passes toward

My Year in Viet Nam

Figqure 6.5
    Using a Chogey Stick to carry a load

Figure 6.6
    Female Work Gang, next to Quarters

My Year in Viet Nam

the enemy forces, and away from the friendly forces, and to keep everything sorted out. He was in radio contact with the friendly ground forces, the fighters, and our radio room. He and the friendly forces could also get some information back and forth by using colored smoke grenades. That was particularly effective in showing the FAC where the friendly troops were.

Sunday morning, Day 42, we were wakened with a call at 0245, asking for help. One of the outposts in our area was under mortar attack. We called for a " Spooky" (C-47 Gunship) from Pleiku, and got Bill Richards airborne toward the area. I went to the radio room to keep track of what was going on.

Everything quieted down after seven rounds of mortar fire. Spooky, ready to use his side firing Gatling guns, arrived and dropped flares. But neither Bill, nor the C-47 crew, nor patrols on the ground could find anything to shoot back at. I went back to bed after an hour and a half, and Bill was an hour or so later.

I must have sung too loudly the previous Sunday. When I went to Mass in the auditorium that morning, Father drafted me to do the readings and lead the singing. Quite a few of the maids and mess attendants were there, as usual, in their Sunday best, beautiful ao dais.

Vietnamese women seemed to bear the burdens of life a lot more than those in other parts of the world. They did the hard labor, like digging, shoveling, and carrying things. To carry a heavy load, they divided it into two equal parts, and suspended it on the ends of specially fitted wooden sticks to lay across their shoulders. I didn't know their name for the carrying sticks, but we called them " chogey sticks". The stick was custom fitted to each owner. They would get the loads attached, then bend their knees and stoop enough to place the chogey sticks across their shoulders. Then they'd stand up and walk away with loads sometimes weighing more than they did. Men used them, too, and even the children had toy chogey sticks. Chogey sticks were probably the most commonly used tool in that part of the world.

Chogey sticks were also a Viet Cong method of moving supplies. They would come into a hamlet in the evening and order everyone to gather with their chogey sticks. Then they'd march off through the night to pick up their loads, leaving the old people and the children at home. They'd go until daylight, then stay under cover until dark, when they'd continue. When their loads were delivered, they'd return to the hamlet, still in the hours of darkness.

The US Army at Qui Nhon had a group of Vietnamese women working as a labor gang. These women, less than five feet tall, were usually guarded by an armed GI at least a foot taller. They dug shallow trenches to lay pipes in, and did all kinds of clean up tasks around the airfield, like sweeping sand up into piles and loading it on trucks to be hauled away. One day they were washing a C-47 that had evidently landed in a muddy field.

The women were most likely using their wages to support themselves and their children while their husbands were in the Army. Surely Vietnamese Army pay did not amount to very much. Our maids were probably better paid than the labor gang.

As noted earlier, we gave our laundry to Mama-san to do. We noted the process. She would pick a bare, clean area of concrete, scrub it and leave it wet. She would spread the clothes on it, wet them, apply soap, and scrub them against the concrete. Finally she would rinse them thoroughly, wring them out, and hang them up to dry. The little bit we paid was surely not very much for all that work.

One night we got a call from a detachment of "Ruff Puffs" (Regional/Provincial Forces) who were encamped on a hilltop for the night, and were being threatened by VC's equipped with a loud speaker, calling on them to surrender or be annihilated. They told the threateners the equivalent of "Go to hell". They dug themselves in, and we had A-1's there at daybreak to support them. That broke up the attack.

On another night, we had a call from an outpost a few miles Southwest of the Bong Son bridges, reporting that they were being mortared. We called Spooky from Pleiku, and it arrived in time to spot mortar tube flashes coming from the attackers. They went into their left turn around the target area and opened up with their Gatling guns firing at it. The mortar fire ceased immediately. The next morning I flew over the camp and talked to the US Army Advisor. He said they had sent a patrol out at daybreak and it found only smashed mortar tubes and bloody body parts.

" Any damage to you folks?" , I asked.

" Yeah, scratch one mess hall" , he replied.

Figure 6.7
    Qui Nhon Flight Line, O-1's Lower Right; Looking
    Across Town and Port Command Supply Area

Figure 6.8
 Ba Gi, 22nd ARVN Headquarters. Note Old Temples, Statue of Buddha Just Below Them, Laterite Runway

CHAPTER VII

GETTING DOWN TO WORK

My life at Qui Nhon began speeding up, and I was finding more and more things to do, with no more time to do them in.

There were just Bill Richards, Bill Coon and I to do the flying. We were not supposed to exceed 85 hours a month flying each, but it looked like we all would. I was supposed to fly only as a secondary job, but we didn't have enough help to afford that luxury. As of the 23rd of August, I had flown all but four days that month.

It turned out that Viet Nam was a land of siesta. A lot of folks took a nap in the afternoon. When the waitresses got the mess hall cleaned up after lunch, they spread their mats out on the floor and took a snooze. The custom was even observed to a degree out in the field.

A sociological observation--there weren't any fat Vietnamese. All the ladies were slender, and the men were mostly quite skinny. Another note, the almost universal wear, out in the rural areas, for other than children, was black pajamas and conical straw hats.

We began experiencing very hot humid days. Those openable side windows in the O-1, allowing scooping the slipstream into one sleeve and out the other, became very much appreciated.

Mama-san was very impressed by the desk and chair that were issued to me, they were " Number One". No safe yet, I really didn't have anything to put in it, anyway.

Mama-san also gained new respect for me on Sunday morning, when she discovered I was Catholic by finding my Rosary under my pillow. She asked me, in sign language, including hands folded as in prayer and pointing to her watch, if I were going to Mass upstairs at eleven o'clock that morning. She assured me that she had gone at nine o'clock at the Qui Nhon Cathedral.

If there were such a thing as a typical day in my career as

an ALO/FAC, it went like this (sometimes):

0630   Up and shave

0700   Breakfast

0730   Target study, and monitor Bill Richards' early flight. Recommend against calling in an air strike on a Viet Cong (or bandit) toll collection set-up Bill saw from the air at a point where the road had been blown up.

1015   Take off and proceed to my assigned target area, scout out the targets.

1100   First flight of three F-100's arrives; I mark the target (some trenches and bunkers), clear the fighters in "Hot", give corrections for their follow on bombing passes and their strafing runs.

1115   Fly over the target to get a Bomb Damage Assessment (BDA), give it to them, thank them, and send them home.

1120 to 1150   Second flight of 3 F-100's arrives, gets briefed on the targets, is directed on the targets, given a BDA, thanked, and sent home.

1150 to 1205   Return to Qui Nhon Airport.

1205 to 1245   Crew Chiefs feed us with barbecued chicken (unusual, but they had it, and had to cook it before it spoiled.)

1245 to 1325   Back to room for notebook and some papers needed for a trip to Nha Trang.

1330   Off on a trip to deliver an O-1 to Nha Trang for Periodic Inspection, and to pick up an airplane from inspection.

1405 to 1445 Stop in Tuy Hoa to discuss business with my FAC there, Capt. Paul Parton.

1445 to 1525 Dodging rain showers to Nha Trang (farther South along the coast).

1605   Off at Nha Trang to return to Qui Nhon

1607 to 1725 Dodging showers and a big rainstorm, returning to Qui Nhon

1800 to 1830 Planning flying schedule for the next day, and taking care of little administrative details. Radio operator Sgt. McIntyre came in to say good-bye, he was returning to the US, his year completed.

1830 to 1900 Shower and change to sports trousers and shirt. Discuss next day's schedule with the line chief.

1900 to 1930 Leisurely dinner (Pork chops, sweet potatoes, peas, vinegared cucumber salad, sheet cake, three tall glasses of iced tea).

1930 to 2030 Read last three issues received of Stars and Stripes (US Armed Forces newspaper). Read the English Edition of the Saigon Newspaper.

2030 to 2130 More business calls, etc.

2130 to 2240 Letter writing.

So there was one (typical?) day's activities. The next day? Up at 0600, shave, etc., etc., planning, take off at 0715 to fly top cover for a ground operation starting at 0815, but first call our bosses at Pleiku for clearance to exceed 85:00 flying time for the month of August. Done.

And so it went, seven days a week.

The end of August briefly turned cool and showery, and we could sleep without the fans on, for a few nights.

My flying had taken a leap for August, had jumped to 90:20. One Bill got 100:00, the other 99:50. All that flying tended to the inflammation of tail bones. We were allowed to fly over one hundred hours in a month only with a special waiver from the 504th Tactical Control Group, our parent unit at Ton Son Nhut.

I had complained (griped?) to my wife that my pillow smelled pretty bad, and that the overhead fan didn't do much good. To my very pleasant surprise, two packages from home arrived on September 1, a nice fluffy pillow with pretty pillow case, and an electric fan! Luxury! And, I was loved!

One indication of the esteem in which the FAC's were held was the fact that they were invited to all the parties. There were two promotion parties the same evening, one for two Army Sergeants, the other for four Army Officers. The Sergeants had broiled hamburgers, chicken and steak, with beer; the Officers had snacks and mixed drinks. Both groups had song fests going, the Sergeants with ukeleles, the Officers with a guitar. Men always had a lot of fun singing together after about two drinks apiece.

We had a variety of problems, the most serious of which was a continuing shortage of pilots. We were averaging two or three flights each, each day. Then there were the extracurricular activities--I found myself the Reader and Song Leader at Mass just about every Sunday morning. That didn't mean I was any good at it, I was just available. I did try to practice ahead of time.

Members of the Republic of Korea Division, (the ROK's), had shopping privileges at the US Army Exchange stores, and when a new one opened in Qui Nhon it looked like about half the Division lined up to get in and buy watches, cameras, radios, etc. I didn't get in line in time to get in the store before closing time that first day.

I found the location of the Military Amateur Radio Station (MARS), and hoped to place a call home on my 18th Wedding Anniversary. The Station was quite near the 85th Evacuation Hospital. But the Station had just moved, and wasn't set up yet. It looked like I'd miss calling on that date, September 7.

When the MARS system worked, we'd place a local telephone call, and the local station would set up radio contact with the MARS station nearest the desired location in the States, Wright-Patterson, for instance, which would then place the local call there, connecting the desired two parties. It was cumbersome, but when it was successful, familiar voices were good to hear.

That day, when I left the MARS station, and came through the 85th's gate, there was a Vietnamese soldier there in US Army Hospital pajamas. The MP's and he asked if I would give his sister, who had been visiting him, a ride back to my part of town. Of course I said,

" Yes."

She looked to be about 40 years old, older than her brother.

Her white ao dai did not fare too well in my dirty Jeep. We tried conversing back and forth in English and French without much success. She showed me where to turn by means of hand signals. After much thought, she finally composed the following sentence in English,

" You Americans are very good".

I answered,

"Thank you. Merci!"

At her destination, she said in English,

"Thank you."

I replied,

"You are welcome."

I did feel I may have added to the favorable American image in Viet Nam, and it was only a block out of my way.

I had been trying in my free(?) time to get our paper work and operating instructions organized. Without an office, everything had been stuffed in little cubbyholes here and there. Some publications we were supposed to have, and didn't, other items were outdated, useless or duplicates. Our inadequate safe was in the radio room.

Lack of manpower continued to plague us. Bill Richards was scheduled to go on R and R (Rest and Recuperation) leave for a week on 23 September, and to return to the States shortly after that, on 17 October.

My need for more help was recognized, finally, when Major Joe Wratten joined us on my 18th Wedding Anniversary, September 7. I flew to Pleiku that day to pick him up. He, the two Bills (Richards and Coon) and I celebrated by having drinks and dinner together. Bill Richards came up with a chilled bottle of wine from somewhere, so, during dinner, we toasted Alberta, and then all our wives.

The Vietnamese Air Force had a limited O-1 operation at the Qui Nhon Airport, which we managed to support to some degree. One day a couple of our pilots and I were standing at our Operations, watching one of their pilots come in to land. To our professional interest, we saw he was in trouble--his tail wheel was cocked at ninety degrees. (It probably had a broken spring.) We could envision a violent ground loop coming up, and had no way to warn him. When he put the tail down, there were some pretty violent gyrations, but, to our relief, he made a successful recovery. Not all the competent pilots were in the USAF.

Division requested me one day to fly VR over the harbor area and along the coast to the North, with a Vietnamese observer. We flew an hour or so, with me trying to point out items and points of significance. But his English wasn't much better than my Vietnamese, so I wasn't sure if we had accomplished his mission or not.

Qui Nhon was a major port for supplies coming in to II Corps. There were always ships at anchor, but a severe shortage of piers, so LST's were used to move goods to shore. From there everything moved Westward, mostly by trucks, largely on Route 19, which passed An Khe, the First US Air Cavalry base, on the way to Pleiku.

CHAPTER VIII

THE WAR SPEEDS UP

The next day, September 10, was a long and busy one. The VC were reported to have threatened that anyone who went to vote on Sunday, the 11th, would be shot. The purpose of the election was to choose delegates to a National Constituent Assembly, whose task it would be to form a democratic central government. The VC had been trying desperately to prevent the election from being held.

After a relatively quiet Thursday and Friday, all hell broke loose early on Saturday morning. Our day began at 0445 with a call reporting that an outpost had been overrun, and to request that we have a FAC overhead the area at 0600. I had one Bill and then the other up flying. I was prepared, after about four hours sleep, to go at 0930. I called our FAC at Cheo Reo, Clarence Rustvold, to come and help out. In spite of the heat in the afternoon, I had the two Bills trying to get some sleep in anticipation of a busy Saturday night and Sunday.

So it went all day long. I flew from 0930 to 1230, and again in the evening, landing after 1930. I had about five hours for the day with Joe Wratten in the back seat. But Bill Coon had flown about 8:00, and Bill Richards about 10:00 for the day. I might have flown even later, had bad weather not moved in. I was prepared to take another flight on Saturday night if we needed one. But after all that activity during the day, Saturday night turned out much quieter.

For Election Day, Sunday, no foreign troops, including us, were permitted in town, or anywhere near the polling places. This was to insure a strictly Vietnamese election. I hoped it would turn out to be a tremendous success, for the sake of the Vietnamese people, who were voting as a step toward setting up a new form of government.

Saturday night turned out to be lots quieter than late Friday night, and Sunday was almost peaceful. Early on Sunday, Lt.

Col. Vong, the Province Chief, was optimistic about a large voter turnout. The VC were trying to keep voters away from the polls so they could say that too few people voted for the election to mean anything. In spite of the VC's threats, it was reported later that nearly ninety percent of the eligible voters had voted.

Our troubles weren't over, of course. The major rice harvest was about to begin, and the VC needed rice to survive. We expected them to try to take some, and our objective was to prevent that from happening.

An odd military problem popped up. The number of ARVN soldiers AWOL (absent without leave) increased. But they were easy to find--they would be back home helping their parents with the rice harvest.

In the middle of Saturday night, our overhead fluorescent lights, which ordinarily wouldn't even come on, began flashing, and the little fan from home, sitting on the chest of drawers, began vibrating very loudly. The combination woke me up. The voltage available to us had increased with the late evening decrease of the numbers of lights and fans in use by others. I got up and turned the light switch off, and adjusted the voltage downward on the transformer supplying my little fan. Then I rolled into bed and went right back to sleep.

There were some more rural roads than the highway, to and from Ba Gi, and I found them more interesting than the same old highroad route. One morning I came upon a man and his wife driving a flock of fifty or more ducks up the road. The man had a long, slender reed, with which he steered the lead duck, to keep them going along the road shoulder instead of in the center of the road or in the ditch. Another morning I saw a seven or eight year old girl bathing her little brother in a stream, sousing him up and down up to his ears, like the laundry. He seemed to be enjoying it immensely.

An interesting feature of the back roads was the bridges replacing those which had been destroyed. Beams were laid across

Figure 8.1
    Steering Ducks

Figure 8.2
    Pierced Steel Planking Bridge

Figure 8.3
   Civic Pride--Hamlet Entrance

Figure 8.4
   Decrepit Bus on Decrepit Highway 1

My Year in Viet Nam

the ditch or canal, then covered with PSP. That was adequate for smaller vehicles, including my Jeep.

The Vietnamese were a handsome people, and, while reserved, they were courteous and responsive. When I bowed and smiled to an elderly man or lady, he or she always bowed in return, with an even bigger smile. The children were the same as everywhere. The little girls would wave, the boys would salute, and they all shouted, even the pantsless little tykes,

" Hey, Joe!", or,

" Okay!"

When I'd walk across the area at Division Headquarters at Ba Gi, the Vietnamese soldiers would greet me with snappy salutes, and,

" Chiao, Trung-ta"!

The little hamlets along the way had their civic pride. Some of them had wrought iron arches over the roads entering their communities, proclaiming each place's name.

However, not all was happiness and joy. Along the main road was a several-classroom school, covered outside with stucco, in a palm tree shaded school yard, perhaps the pride of the community. It also had its sad side. I was told that some time previously, while classes were in session, the VC had come, and ordered the children and the teachers out of the building, then cut them down with AK-47 rifle fire. Their parting words reportedly were,

" Maybe this will teach your parents to cooperate with us!"

I had gotten used to seeing people turned to the side of the road to relieve themselves. One time I met a rickety old bus stopped along the road, while the passengers all got off for a pit stop.

One day I was giving some Vietnamese soldiers a ride to town when we met a woman, probably in her thirties, in our lane. I turned to the other lane to miss her, and when we got to thirty or forty feet from her, she raised her black pajama top to expose her breasts to our view as we passed. I glanced at the soldier beside me, and he looked very embarrassed, probably because a Vietnamese woman had acted so vulgarly before an American.

I certainly was flying enough, and was in excellent health except for my sitter, which didn't seem to be developing callouses fast enough. After all our flying on Saturday, Joe Wratten was almost checked out, and on Monday I was able to release Rustvold back to Cheo Reo.

Day 64, September 9, had provided an interesting adventure. I was on my usual run up Highway 1, when, Lo! and Behold! The VC had set up, just outside a little hamlet, a barrier across the road, and were collecting tolls or taxes from (or just plain robbing), every one coming along. I circled left on the side of the road away from the hamlet, and the collectors went into the brush beside the road. I dropped a yellow smoke grenade, and everyone scattered. I circled to the right for another pass. That took me directly over the little hamlet. As I flew over it, I suddenly heard what sounded like loud popcorn popping.

I was being shot at!

The noise continued for about thirty seconds, while I zigged and zagged and began a climb to a thousand feet higher. There were no more shots, and I couldn't tell where the firing had come from, so there was no point in calling in an air strike.

A while later, Bill Richards flew over the same area, got shot at, and spotted exactly where the fire was coming from. An ARVN artillery unit was nearby, so Bill called in and spotted for their fire on the unfriendly folks. That silenced them.

I wrote a letter to my ALO boss, Lt. Col. Scroggin, at Pleiku, requesting five more FAC's, with a courtesy copy to Col. Hunter, Senior Advisor of the 22nd Advisory Group, confirming my earlier verbal requests. Col. Hunter thought it was a good letter.

On the evening of the 14th of September, we had a little excitement on the beach next to our compound. A guard near the beach saw someone swimming toward the shore. When challenged, the swimmer turned and swam farther out. The guard started shooting. The emergency defense team scurried around, there were more shots, plus flares, until everybody found out what was going on. Then things quieted down. I never found out what happened to the swimmer.

One of my maintenance single airmen came and asked for my permission for him to live in downtown Qui Nhon. Apparently a girl he liked lived near there, and he had become friends with the family who would rent the room to him. He would plan to continue taking his meals in the military mess. The maintenance chief, M/Sgt. Keim, had already taken a look at the room he would occupy, and said it was decent. I told the airman to find the regulations governing living " on the economy" and bring them to me; if the regulations did not prohibit it, I'd give my permission.

Like everyone else, I began calling the Viet Cong "Charlie".

My complaints about how hot the foam rubber mattresses were brought a package from Anna Mary Landauer, Alberta's sister. It was a cotton mattress pad. I began to think all the ladies loved me. I started to put it on my bed, but Mama-san came in about that time, saw what I was doing, and wouldn't let me finish it, and she was determined to do it all by herself. Men are such stumblebums, they don't know how to make a bed!

Women are all alike.

The weather turned a little cooler, if one can call ninety degrees cooler, and the main rice harvest began. I observed that the farmers evidently traded help around just as they used to do in Kansas. From the air I would see ten or fifteen of them working in one paddy. Most of the paddies were not more than an acre. They'd cut the rice using hand sickles, tie it in small bundles with wisps of straw, put several bundles on each end of a chogey stick, balance it on their shoulders, then carry it to the house. After it had dried for a while, they'd thresh it by beating the top

Figure 8.5
   Harvesting Rice

Figure 8.6
   Carrying the Rice to the House

Figure 8.7
    Threshing the Rice

Figure 8.8
    Country Cottage, thatched rice straw roof, walls of mud covered straw.

ends of the bundles on a tilted lattice they stood behind, something like a wash board. This part seemed to be done mostly by the women. The rice was gathered from under the lattice, and sometimes further dried by spreading it on a clean surface, such as a spot on the road!! The straw was then sold or used by the farmer for making roofs or sidewalls of buildings, which the vulgar Americans called hooches.

The cooler and damper weather encouraged the mosquitos, so that we used our mosquito nets around our beds. The Hospital had a few malaria patients, but I was hopeful that my weekly malaria pill would ward that off.

The question of shooting at known enemies with the M-16 we each carried in flight came up. The chance of hitting anything from 1500 feet was pretty remote, and flying lower would expose us to a lot more damaging fire than we could put out. Therefore, don't do it. The subject never surfaced again.

As my tenth week out of the states faded away, the approaching monsoon season was heralded by still a little cooler weather, showers, and decreased visibility. I didn't really mind. On Saturday, September 16, I passed 50:00 flying time for September. It looked like I wouldn't miss 100:00 by too much.

The US First Air Cavalry Division began conducting an operation in Binh Dinh Province, so my tactical area of responsibility was somewhat diminished for a while. They shortly had captured a few VC, a large store of grenades and ammunition, a large store of rice, and a grenade factory. I wished them much continued good luck.

That Sunday when I went to fly, it had rained, and the road around the end of the runway had about an inch of very sloppy reddish brown mud on it. I saw a lady walking along the side of the road who had obviously slipped and fallen on her sitter, in her black pajamas. I *really* felt sorry for her when I saw that she was going to be a Momma. I tried not to splash mud on her or anyone else as I drove along. When I came back from flying, the mud had turned mostly to dust.

Just across the barbed wire and the road around the end of the runway was an area of unbelievably decrepit shacks,

My Year in Viet Nam

Figure 8.9
    Around the End of the Qui Nhon Runway

Figure 8.10
    Children at Home in Qui Nhon

obviously built of anything that came to hand, paste board, sides of packing crates, pieces of plywood, large cans that had been opened up and placed to help shed rain, and so on. And people lived in them, perhaps refugees from the ROK cleared area.

Along with the other aviation activities using the Qui Nhon Airport was Air Viet Nam (or similar name). Every day there would be a DC-3 parked in front of their terminal (hardly as big as the airplane) on their small ramp just off the end of the runway.

Father (Lt. Col.) Miller had come to rely so much on me to do the readings and lead the singing at the eleven o'clock Mass on Sunday, that a real crisis would ensue if I ever had to fly at that time.

Monday night I had an overnight guest, Lt. Col. Charles V. Gibson. He was one of my classmates at Hurlburt, and was now the 24th Special Zone ALO at Kontum. One reason for his visit was to see if he could persuade me to trade positions with him. He thought we were having all the fun chasing the VC in Binh Dinh Province. I told him I'd think about it, but made no promises.

I had an inquiry from home about where we stopped for gas when we were out flying. Well, most of our airplanes could easily fly about four hours between gas stops, and our usual missions were seldom more than three and a half. The particular airplane I flew most of the time could go almost six hours, maybe because when I was just out looking, or was directing an air strike, I kept the engine throttled back. It helped that some of the outposts where we landed had aviation gas in barrels, and hand pumps to transfer it to airplanes, if needed.

I had to explain also that when I reported that an outpost had been overrun, it meant that it had been captured by the Viet Cong or the North Vietnamese Army (NVA).

I was wishing I could converse in Vietnamese. I would have greatly enjoyed being able to go out and talk to some of the Vietnamese farmers. What a wonderful time I'd have had, getting their views on government, society in general, and how to grow things. Farmers are supposed to be hicks, but I didn't believe it.

The hicks I knew came from big cities. It takes a smart man (or woman) to coax a living from the soil, and farmers know the value of hard work.

Another mattress pad came, this one from Alberta's Mom, via Sears-Roebuck. The squeaky wheel was really getting the grease!

Another operation by the 22nd ARVN was set to begin on Thursday. We scheduled 3.5 hours of flying each, but that was only a guess about how much our help would be needed.

The 41st Regiment of the 22nd supported a convoy up Highway 1 to English Field, North of the Bong Son, to resupply our troops there, on Thursday. Leading the unit were bulldozers to fill in the VC's hand dug trenches across the road. The operation got almost half way, and encamped for the night. Before daylight next morning, it was attacked by a force of the NVA. Our guys dug in their heels, fought like tigers, and called us for air support. We had A-1's overhead at daylight and broke up the attack. The enemy scattered toward the hills to the West. I flew over the area about mid morning, and saw some of the " bad guys" sneaking into a hooch. I aimed a Willy Pete into it, and didn't see any more of them. I suspected it might be a tunnel entrance. I finished up the day with 8:05, kind of a long one.

Division asked the First Cav to use their helicopters to put blocking forces in position to keep the enemy troops from fleeing into and over the hills to the West, while the 41st's forces tried to scarf them up. On Friday and Saturday no First Cav blocking forces appeared. On Sunday the area was swarming with them, but by that time all the enemy forces had " dee-deed" (run away). The convoy continued on its resupply mission. When it got to the Bong Son, it had to cross it on the railroad bridge-- the Highway 1 bridge had been destroyed some time before.

I had noted that whenever active fighting was going on, the local populace fled Southward. They were sheltered in temporary Red Cross marked tents, or in somewhat more permanent long metal roofed buildings.

Figure 8.11
 Bong Son River Bridges--Highway Bridge, two spans out, Railroad Bridge used for the Highway

Figure 8.12
 Refugee Temporary Camp, Some Red, SomeWhite Tent Tops

Bill Richards went on R & R, and wouldn't be available for much flying when he got back; his date for rotation back to the States was imminent.

On Sunday, Day 78, we got a new FAC, Lt. Darryl Dixon. He was scheduled to replace Bill Richards. Another man was promised to come soon, and then I'd be able to let Joe Wratten go to Tuy Hoa, where he was scheduled to go in the first place.

Because we flew lots of air strikes, we found ourselves in the business of checking out new FAC's on their way to other units. One came from our parent unit at Nha Trang on Thursday, flew with us on Friday and Saturday, and returned to Nha Trang that Sunday. We also agreed with the ROK's ALO that we'd support him for his FAC check outs. A new FAC would ride in the back seat for one strike mission, then direct air strikes from the front seat while an experienced FAC rode in the back seat.

During siesta time at Ba Gi one day, I made my way up to the top of the hill, and took some pictures of those very old temples, or whatever they were. They were built of bricks, without mortar, except where there were some recent repairs. Their only apparent current use was for sight-seeing by the Allied forces. From there I continued down the hill on the other side and took some pictures of the traditional very large seated Buddha. Beyond that was Ba Gi's laterite runway.

I drove the back road returning to Qui Nhon, and took a picture of a girl about eleven or twelve years old, in her conical straw hat, carrying a woven basket, probably on an errand for her mother. And I got a picture of a boy about the same age with his bicycle. I had a vision of the two growing up and living happily ever after in a peaceful Viet Nam. The boy kind of spoiled the mood by asking for a cigarette.

A lot of people who did not look like they could afford it smoked cigarettes. Perhaps it was no worse than chewing betel nut. The mouths of some of the old ladies who chewed it looked like black holes. They did look like they had no cares, smiling a lot. I guessed betel nut had that effect.

The children acted like little kids everywhere, with a special attraction to dirt. A mud puddle was especially intriguing

Figure 8.13
 Old Chinese Temple, Hill above Ba Gi

Figure 8.14
 Statue of Buddha at Ba Gi--Note Swastika

My Year in Viet Nam

Figure 8.15
Girl on an Errand

Figure 8.16
Boy with His Bicycle

to boys, just had to be waded in.

Little boys were more boisterous than the girls, jumping around a lot. The little girls, especially if nicely dressed, tried to look like young ladies. A little boy, being led by the hand, or carried, was always looking to see where they had been, rather than where they were going.

On Tuesday, I flew part of the top cover for the 41st returning down Highway 1 from their trip the previous week. We didn't want the VC to ambush them. Actually that particular stretch of road had been secure since the fighting the previous Friday.

With two days left to go in September, I had passed 90:00 hours of flying for the month. Probably I could avoid overshooting a hundred. (Actually I got another two and a half.)

Ever since the fighting the previous week I had been distressed about the NVA's bodies still lying where they fell in the fighting on Friday. Out of human decency they should have been buried days earlier.

As I flew over the area again on this particular day, I saw a fresh grave beside where each body had lain. The poor farmers returning to their paddies had done the sad duty. But the mothers, wives and children in North Viet Nam would never know where their loved ones were buried. That was especially sad because it was very important in that part of the world to know where one's ancestors were buried.

Another sad event happened that day. Bill Coon was flying overhead and saw it all. A civilian bus and a Vietnamese Army truck were meeting on Highway 1, about 20 miles Northwest of Qui Nhon, not far from Phu Cat. Just as they met, a Communist land mine detonated under the bus, and blew it over on top of the truck. Two people were killed, and quite a few were injured. It also blew a large hole in the road bed. After the bus was rolled off the truck, the truck drove away under its own power.

The bus was still there when I flew over the site about five o'clock in the evening. It looked like the whole front end had been blown off it. The mine must have been set off from a hidden location nearby. The truck passing at the same time must have been just a coincidence. This act did not seem to me to be useful in helping persuade the South Vietnamese people to sympathize with the Viet Cong.

We had a bit of a diversion one day. One of our FAC's forgot to check the security of his oil filler cap on preflight, and a short time into his flight had oil all over the front of his airplane. He managed to land at Phu Cat, about 20 miles out on Highway 1, and we flew some oil out to him. We all had a lesson learned.

I received an invitation from Dai-ta (Col.) Hieu, the 22nd's Commander, to attend the official ceremonies at 1000 hours on Saturday, October 1, and the party at noon, celebrating the eleventh anniversary of the founding of the 22nd Infantry Division (ARVN), at Division Headquarters at Ba Gi. Another invitation came, from Gen. Meyer, Commander of the Army Support Command, (mentioned earlier), to attend the dedication ceremonies for the new Support Command Chapel, at 1400 on October 7. Both were in the nature of Command Performances, so I planned to attend.

I spent all day Friday at Ba Gi, in a continued series of briefings and meetings planning for a big operation to begin on Sunday the second of October. It was to involve all the Allied Forces operating in Binh Dinh Province. Those included the 22nd ARVN, the Vietnamese 3rd Airborne Brigade, the ROK Capital Division, US B-52's, the US First Air Cavalry Division, and others. Because the area was under the military jurisdiction of the 22nd ARVN, Col. Hieu was in overall command. The First Cav's Commander, a Major General, started taking charge, saying how everything was going to be done, but Col. Hieu very politely, nevertheless firmly, said,

" No, Sir, this is the way it will be done."

The General sat quietly through the rest of the briefings.

The upcoming joint effort was called Operation Irving. The plans and the briefings were Classified SECRET until Sunday morning, when the execution of the ground portion of the plan was scheduled to begin.

Bill Richards returned from his R & R to Hong Kong, and brought the two tape recorders I had asked him to. They were to provide some voice communication with my family in Ohio, via tapes to be mailed back and forth. Bill also said there were some very good buys in all kinds of things. I began considering Hong Kong as a possible place to go on my R & R, still months away,

The celebration of the Eleventh Anniversary of the founding of the 22nd ARVN, on Saturday, October 1, at Ba Gi, was a memorable affair.

Before the official opening of the program, a Vietnamese H-19 helicopter, with Vietnamese pilot and his American Counterpart, was making low passes past the row of flagpoles, with all the Allies' flags, on the slope behind the parade ground and reviewing stand. On one pass, they got too close to the flagpoles and clipped one of them with their tail rotor. It shattered and instantaneously left them with no anti-torque control with their rudder pedals. The aircraft began an immediate counter rotation, but the American pilot promptly closed the throttle and dumped the collective. They made a hard landing just a bit beyond the slope behind the flags. No one on the ground or in the chopper was hurt, but one landing gear strut was badly bent.

The main event went on as planned. There were speeches, presentations of medals (pinned on by high school girls in their long black hair and white ao dais), firing of cannon, promotions, and Karate demonstrations by Korean soldiers. They broke boards, tiles, and bricks with their bare hands and feet--and even with their heads (using several layers of towels for padding).

The Ba Gi Officers' Club was not impressive at all compared with US standards. It had a bar and lounge in one end of a long building, with a dining area toward the other end. The kitchen apparently was at the far end.

There was a several course luncheon, served to us, with our choices of drinks. While we were eating, an orchestra played, and four different Vietnamese girls sang songs for us. They sounded beautiful, but I didn't understand a word.

Honored guests were Major General Vinh Loch, II Corps Commander, and a Vietnamese Army Lt. General whose name I did not learn. I thought Col. Hieu was the best looking, probably

Figure 8.17
Karate Demonstration--Leap over Seven to Split the Board

Figure 8.18
Awards Being Pinned on by High School Girls

the best educated, and likely to go far.

The event was partly in celebration of the recent victories of the 22nd ARVN in the field, and the decorations and promotions grew out of those successes.

In preparation for the morrow's launching of Operation Irving, the B-52's had been dropping bombs on the Phu Cat Mountains North of Qui Nhon for a couple of days. We could hear them exploding throughout the day, and even from my room, in the evening hours. We couldn't see the airplanes flying over, they were so high. The ROK's began moving into and on top of the Phu Cats when the bombing stopped.

The Phu Cats were known to harbor large numbers of Viet Cong, and unfortunately for them, their families.

It began to rain in the evening, was that good or bad news for the beginning of Operation Irving? Conventional knowledge propounded by the news media in the States was that the Allied Forces in Viet Nam did poorly in the Monsoon Season.

CHAPTER IX

OPERATION IRVING

Very early on the morning of October 2, the Allied Forces took up their positions to begin Operation Irving. The objective was to clear enemy forces out of an area bounded on the West by Highway 1, on the East by the South China Sea, on the South by the Phu Cats, and on the North by another range of hills.

The ARVN forces were deployed along Highway 1 during the night and early in the morning, the ROK's continued moving into the Phu Cats; the First Cav took up blocking positions in the rugged terrain along the North side of the area. At 0700 the ARVN forces began sweeping to the East from the highway, searching thoroughly as they went, meeting some resistance. The blocking forces prevented escape to either the North or the South, and closed in on the area as the operation progressed.

My job as ALO was to coordinate air support for the ARVN forces, and for others on an as needed basis. That included having a FAC over the area when the weather was fit, and being able to call for air strikes if and when needed.

To get in position from which to operate, I flew out to Phu Cat, twenty or so miles Northwest of Qui Nhon, at the West end of the Phu Cat Mountains, where the Command Post for the operation was set up, early on Sunday morning. Phu Cat was a training base for the Regional and Popular (Provincial) Forces, something like the National Guard in the US. It had training facilities and a short air strip.

The US Army provided the Fire Coordination Center. It was equipped quite well, with power units, telephones, radios, field kitchens housed in trailer trucks, and various sizes of tents for various purposes. Much of it was transportable by helicopter. Small portable radios provided rapid communications between units on the ground and with aircraft. This whole set up was miles from any fighting.

I was assigned to one Jamesway tent with all my necessary communications gear, and shared a sleeping tent with an Army

My Year in Viet Nam

Lt. Col. We each had a bunk, (an Army steel cot, with air mattress). I had taken along my toilet kit, change of clothes, a sheet, and my latest mattress cover from Mom Doege, so I was really quite comfortable. The food was good, and plentiful.

The mud was plentiful, too.

The weather was bad and got worse, with periods of rain all day long. I had FAC's providing top cover when the weather permitted, but we had no calls for fighter support. I answered a few phone calls, and talked on the radio a bit, but other than that just watched it rain. After a restful night, I flew back to Qui Nhon next morning, and Bill Coon went out to relieve me.

On return, I forgot to take along my bag with toilet kit, so when I flew in the afternoon I stopped in to get it, and to leave a letter for Bill. So far, so good, but when I taxied out for take off, one magneto would not check properly. I taxied back in, and we tried to fix it, without success. So I stayed another night, on a folding cot, with mosquito net but no bedding. That was not nearly so comfortable as the first night. Mechanics spent all the next day working on the airplane. It still did not get back to Qui Nhon. But I did, anyway. On Wednesday we finally got our sick airplane back, flyable again.

Odd thoughts, while it was raining, and there was not much else to do--the names of ordinary soldiers change with the wars. World War I infantrymen were called doughboys, in World War II they were known as GI's, in Viet Nam they often were called "grunts". The titles of females vary, too. In Viet Nam, American ladies were called "round eyes", while the Vietnamese girls were sometimes called "slopes", for their slanted (folded) eyelids.

Thursday came along, and Operation Irving continued. It seemed like a very successful operation to this point. Quite a few prisoners were being taken, and not many enemy troops were being killed. There was not a news reporter in sight, so perhaps the folks back home wouldn't even hear about it.

I had been trading off the forward operating position with Majors Bill Coon and Joe Wratten. In five days we hadn't been asked to provide any air strikes, but when the weather permitted we had a FAC over the combat area.

The Northeast Monsoon had apparently arrived, but instead of hindering our operation, it had helped. The VC tended to dig a lot of tunnels as hiding places and bases of operations, but they were being driven to the surface by the flooding of the tunnels. They were more easily found, then.

The ROK's rounded up prisoners in the Phu Cats, including women and children, driven out of their caves by the B-52 bombing. It was reported that most of them were pale from having been underground out of the sun for so long.

I missed the dedication of the new Support Command Chapel.

With some of our Intelligence staff, I visited the prisoner compound where the captives taken in Operation Irving were kept. Most of them looked dejected, but they were being pretty well treated, I thought. There were a number of women prisoners. One of them was a 17-year old girl who freely admitted, in fact, bragged, that she was the leader of a group of 30 women guerillas. There was also a North Vietnamese girl who was a nurse. She looked confused and sad, and jumped quickly to do things for the 17-year old.

All the people picked up with weapons or in uniform were considered Viet Cong or NVN. The NVN tag was verified by their accent; the Southerners readily recognized them by their speech.

Quite a few others were suspects. They were screened and questioned, to identify the VC among them. Those about whom there was some doubt were sent to the district chief, who had people on his staff from every hamlet, who could identify the VC members. Cleared suspects were sent home.

There were not many women, so those who were only suspects were kept with the known VC. One of the suspects I judged to be in her late forties was in tears. The Sergeant in charge assured her, through an interpreter, that she could soon go back to her village. Some of the women were cooks, laundresses and so on, for the VC troops. One of them had her little boy, about six, with her. Her husband had not yet been captured.

The men identified as VC were sent to a prison camp near Pleiku, where, I heard, they were taught a trade from which to make a living, and then released The people cleared of suspicion were taken back to their hamlets or to a refugee center. I felt sorry for all of them, especially the 17-year old girl.

Saturday was Day 91, and we acquired another FAC, Major Jack Henry, who came from a maintenance job at Phan Rang. He came at a good time, since Bill Richards was due to leave for the States the next day. But Jack had a DEROS for January, so we'd have him less than three months.

We'd seen very little action in our post at Phu Cat, all we were getting there was experience. So I sent Lt. Dixon out, he needed experience as much as any of us.

My tour in SEA was 1/4 over!

My Absentee Ballot came from Rapid City, South Dakota, so I voted, and mailed it back.

A newly assigned intelligence officer--had arrived only the day before--rode in the back seat with me, and did not get sick, though he did report feeling a bit uncomfortable. He was to replace a man about to retire. I had tried to treat him as gently as possible, I didn't need a messy airplane. At least he got a look at some of the things we were always checking out for their possible intelligence value.

Secretary McNamara came by on Columbus Day to see how Operation Irving had been doing. I was off on a trip to Pleiku, Cheo Reo and Tuy Hoa, so he didn't get a chance to talk to me.

As Operation Irving wound down, a display was set up in Qui Nhon showing some of the large quantities of materiel captured. There were many weapons, supplies of ammunition, medical supplies, and various other items the VC in the area had been using to support their efforts. And much of that had been carried on human shoulders from North Viet Nam.

Another new FAC came in that day, and another was expected the next day. That would allow two FAC's each at Tuy Hoa and Cheo Reo, and four besides me at Qui Nhon. That was expected to help us catch up on some of the things that hadn't been getting done, and none of us would have to fly so much. One more man would let each of us take one day a week off. What a way to fight a war! Maybe I could even do some local shopping.

A new and disturbing possible change in policy came up, not yet confirmed. Anyway, it was announced that to maintain continuity and high experience level of the Advisory teams, certain key personnel, such as Senior Advisors and Liaison Officers would have their tours extended to 24 months, in order to maintain continued high quality support of the war effort. The policy was to apply to personnel already in Viet Nam, as well as to those to be assigned in the future.

I had three hopes to fall back on:
1. The new policy would not apply to Air Force Officers.
2. I was not really a key person.
3. The policy would not apply to people in actual combat.

My newest FAC was Major Curtis Love. On Friday I rode in the back seat with him up front, in the process of checking him out in our operation. On Friday I sent Joe Wratten to Tuy Hoa. He outranked Capt. Paul Parton, who had been alone in the FAC job there. In another week I planned to send Darryl Dixon to Cheo Reo to join Clarence Rustvold. That would leave Majors Love, Coon, Moore and Henry with me in Qui Nhon.

On Sunday afternoon, I flew an airplane to Nha Trang, about a hundred miles down the coast, to get a 100-hour inspection on Monday. That evening I had an hour long visit with Major Nelson Flack, from my old days with the B-58 flight control system. Nels was Operations Officer in a Psychological Warfare operation, flying C-47's and U-10's. He thought it was an interesting endeavor, but it didn't involve much fighting. They dropped leaflets and operated loud speakers, over the opposing forces, urging the Viet Cong to surrender, or " chieu hoy".

I had sent Joe Wratten to Tuy Hoa on Friday, and here he was on Monday with an airplane for inspection also.

Bill Coon had been sick for a couple of days, and on

My Year in Viet Nam

Figure 9.1
Front and Back of a "Chieu Hoy" Leaflet

Sunday morning went on sick call with a very sore throat. He was admitted to Intensive Care. I was worried about him, and a little reluctant to leave that day. The doctor didn't seem to know what his illness was. I hoped none of the rest of us would catch it.

My airplane wasn't ready yet Monday evening, so I had another nice visit with Nels Flack. He was short handed, like about everyone else. We discussed the possibility of their helping out in the 22nd's area of operations.

I got back to base on Tuesday. Bill Coon was grounded until he could get a physical at Langley Field after his return Stateside. That left me as the most experienced FAC still flying out of Qui Nhon.

I received a clipping from Time Magazine from home that finally had something to say about Operation Irving. The news story almost completely left out the major parts played by 22nd ARVN's and ROK Capital Division's soldiers. The accompanying picture was authentic, it was a scene at Phu Cat.

The ARVN had captured more VC than had the First Cav. I didn't hear any figures for the ROK's. I suspected that the article was written at First Cav's headquarters in An Khe.

My suspicion was confirmed later when I got a copy of Time's Overseas Edition about Irving. It made no mention of all the preplanning that had gone into the Operation, and said it all began sort of by accident when a Huey was shot down over a hamlet along the North edge of the area. That item destroyed forever my faith in the accuracy of Time Magazine's news articles.

Oh, the Huey was shot down, all right, I thought because the pilot was flying stupidly low.

I finally had three majors, Henry, Love and Moore actively flying as FAC's at Qui Nhon, and in a few days would take Dixon to Cheo Reo. We still had Coon, but he was grounded for medical reasons.

Flying could still be enough of a challenge to be interesting. On Thursday evening, Day 103, I flew through fog, low clouds and rain, dodging old Chinese temples, hills and helicopters, to land at six o'clock, just five minutes before the field closed. The heavy rain continued all night.

On Friday, we flew only one of five scheduled flights, and on Saturday we couldn't fly at all. The Monsoon had really set in, in earnest. I had taken Darryl Dixon's B-4 bag to Cheo Reo on Wednesday, and planned to take him on Saturday; no such luck.

In my conversations with Darryl, I discovered he was an Outstanding ROTC Graduate, in Electrical Engineering, at Oklahoma State. He hoped to study Astronautical Engineering at AFIT, my most recent Alma Mater. Of course I cheered that!

Col. Hunter, the Senior US Army Advisor in the Qui Nhon area, made me feel complimented and appreciated. He said he had told Lt. Col. Scroggin, my ALO boss at Pleiku, that I had been doing a fine job. It was a big morale boost to know that my efforts were appreciated.

We had been having so few air strikes that I couldn't get my two newest FAC's checked out. Jack Henry had had only one flight, and Curt Love, one. We finally were scheduled for two on the next Thursday, so I programmed a back seat ride for me with each of them. Meanwhile, our marvelous public utility system managed to delete our bathroom from the lighting circuit, projecting a shave in the dark for the next morning.

Probably we should have felt privileged above measure. Out in the hamlets and the countryside, there was no electricity, except by flashlight or electric lantern. What lighting there was, was by kerosene lamps, or perhaps by a few Coleman gasoline lanterns. Nearly everyone lived in small hamlets or villages, there were very few isolated farmsteads. Perhaps that was because the rural people liked company.

I began making plans for my return to the States the next July. I would fly, courtesy of the Air Force, to meet my wife in Honolulu, spend some time there, then catch a Space A trip on a ship to San Francisco. There we would take delivery on a new Volkswagen Fastback, and then drive back to Ohio, with leisurely visits on the way. Optimistic, wasn't I?

Bill Coon still didn't know what he'd had. Perhaps it

was a combination of a bad cold and a cholera shot. In any case, he continued grounded. He was to leave Qui Nhon for home on about November 12.

Two flights on Thursday, the first fighter strikes in ten days or more, finished Jack Moore's check out, and left one flight to go for Curt Love.

It was magical how a full moon, a soft breeze in the palms, and gentle waves from the shimmering water lapping at the sandy beach, could transform our setting into a romantic place. But when daylight came, it revealed the dirt and drabness of our realities.

On Saturday we had another fighter strike to direct, so Curt Love completed his check out. I expected another FAC in the near future, and possibly another O-1.

Jack Moore, my newly checked out Division FAC, (replacing Bill Coon), and I were talking, and he mentioned spending two cold winters in South Dakota. We discovered, to our mutual amazement, that not only had we been at Ellsworth AFB at the same time, but that we had lived in the same small (four units) apartment building, and our wives knew each other, of course. Small world! I guessed we hadn't recognized each other sooner because over 14 years or so we both had become more challenged in the hair and scalp departments.

Bill Coon was feeling fine again, and very cheerful, no more flying to get shot at, and less than two weeks from starting home. Hooray!

A very big event was scheduled for Tuesday, the first of November, (Day 115). It was Viet Nam National Day, celebrating the birth of the Nation on All Saints Day in 1954. I had received a printed invitation, with a reserved seat in the main reviewing stand, representing the US Air Force. Beside me to my left were other military officers and civilian dignitaries. Over our heads was a roof to keep the sun and rain off. I could see everything, and the parade route was right to left in front of me. On the other side of the parade route from me was a row of flags, representing all the nations supporting South Viet Nam against the

Communists. I had just about the "best seat in the house".

The program began with a welcoming and celebratory speech by Trung-ta (Lt. Col.) Vong, the Province Chief. Since it was all in Vietnamese, I didn't understand any of it.

Dai-ta (Col.) Hieu's speech was also in Vietnamese, but we English speakers were provided a typed English translation of it.

He began:

"The first of November is a very great day in the history of the Republic of Viet Nam. On this day, 3 years ago, the Armed Forces, with the strong support of the people, had overthrown a dictatorial regime and assumed the task of leading the nation, in order to achieve an early victory over Communism and rebuild the country.

"Reviving these historical moments, we cannot forget the contributions of the soldiers of the Republic who have died for the Revolution.

"As the Commanding Officer of the 22nd Infantry Division and the 22nd Division Tactical Area, I respectfully bow my head before the disembodied spirits of the heroes who have sacrificed their lives for the Just Cause, and I wish to extend my heartfelt gratitude to all military and civilian cadres for having smashed corruption and autocracy to safeguard the survival of the Vietnamese people, revealing a new horizon of genuine democracy and freedom."

He noted the many successes of the Allied Armed Forces in the 22nd Division's Tactical Area and throughout the country, and pointed out that the Viet Cong had been suffering one defeat after another. In the last three months, thousands of Viet Cong had been killed, and hundreds of their weapons seized. With the continuous assistance from Allied Forces, the war situation was very satisfactory, and going better than expected.

In the political domain, the National Directory (Central Government) had been enlarged to include 10 civilians, representing various social, political and religious groups, and it had been decided to form a new committee called the Army and People's Council to advise the government.

The greatest success of the Central Government was the election of the National Constituent Assembly, in a manner completely free of pressure. It was the first step towards a more democratic government, which he hoped would provide time to carry out the goals of the Revolution, and give the Allies a better opportunity to help the country, which for so long had been demolished by war.

The Election, on September 11, in which 94.2% of the 301,054 eligible voters in Binh-Dinh, Phu-Yen and Phu-Bon Provinces cast ballots, had eloquently shown the entire world, as well as the common enemy, that the South Vietnamese people had chosen only freedom and democracy.

In response to the earlier appeal of the authorities, a great number of rural people had left their villages, and moved to secure areas where they could live safely. The Viet Cong thus lost the people's support, and their defeats had lowered and shaken their morale. The friendly forces were destroying the VC organization from the highest to the lowest rank. And, the Monsoon was no longer to the Viet Cong's advantage.

The Pacification and Rural Reconstruction program was well under way, allowing many displaced people to move back into their homes. It promised to become the decisive factor in restoration of the homeland, and wipe out the strongholds of the Viet Cong.

"--The problem of war refugees has imposed another burden on our shoulders. With endurance and self-confidence in our determination to bring the Red Scourge to an end, we have overcome all difficulties and obstacles. We have established more than 70 new life hamlets, a great number of elementary schools, wells, dispensaries and communal roads, providing our fellow-countrymen with ample opportunities and means of communication to satisfy their daily needs and improve their economy.

" In a word, with magnificent exploits on the battlefront, and consolidation of internal affairs in the rear, the combatants of the 22nd Division Tactical Area have raised their unit banners high, and contributed a great part to the defense of their

Figure 9.2
    Abandoned Hamlet and Farming Area, Grown up to Weeds

Figure 9.3
    Refugee Shelters, Country Church Yard

My Year in Viet Nam

Figure 9.4
    Inhabited Hamlet and Farming Area

Fatherland."

He pointed out that many difficulties and obstacles still remained. The Communist Vietnamese had not yet laid down their arms. So, in 1967, greater hardships and tremendous effort awaited, before final victory could be achieved.

He continued,

"We do not promote war but we cannot accept a humiliating capitulation. We are a peace-loving people. But the peace we desire is a peace in honor, a legitimate peace, in which our national sovereignty and the integrity of our territory are strictly respected. We will protest against all movements or peace talks that could betray the supreme rights of our people. We will go on fighting through all hardships. We will meet many challenges. But we will not be alone in the struggle. Our Allies, despite great expenditures, dangers, loss of their loved ones, will help us eliminate the Communist aggressors, the mortal enemy of mankind's progress.

" In celebrating this 1966 National Day, I would like to extend my deep gratitude to all US and Korean comrades-in-arms for having cooperated and fought side by side with us in this noble mission to protect our borders. I also express the hope that with the selfless devotion of the fighting men of the Free World forces in conjunction with the eternal tradition of our valorous people, the goals of our Revolution will be accomplished in a spirit of solidarity.

"Certainly," he concluded, "the final victory will be ours.

" Thank you."

Then the parade began. As everywhere, everyone, especially the children, watched in awe. There were various groups, the military units, with their equipment, trucks, weapons carriers, and marching men in uniform. I found the APC's with brightly painted large white sidewall tires amusing, they looked like big gunnery targets. The fuel and water trucks, even the fire trucks, did their bit.

But what I liked the best were the various non military groups, high school boys in black trousers and white shirts, high school girls in white ao dais, with black hair to their waists. There was also a large group of Pacification Team Members in distinctive brown uniforms something like our Future Farmers of America. Their work was to help resettle the hamlets.

There were some airplane flyovers, and the children's eyes all turned skyward, they were completely entranced.

Figure 9.5
    Parade Watchers; An Aircraft Flew Over

My Year in Viet Nam

Figure 9.6
Flags of Viet Nam (Center) and its Allies

Figure 9.7
High School Boys

My Year in Viet Nam

Figure 9.8
High School Girls

Figure 9.9
APC--Those Wheels Look Like Targets!

My Year in Viet Nam

Figure 9.10
Pacification Team Members Next in Parade
(Flat Top Fatigue Caps Worn by ROK Troops)

CHAPTER X

THE STRUGGLE GOES ON

The war went on, as Col. Hieu had predicted. On November 3, Day 117, I flew two high-bladder-pressure flights totaling almost seven hours. I surely wished that that O-1 had some kind of relief facilities. The weather was cooler than it had been, which I appreciated.

In the evening I had an interesting visit with US Army Major Johnson. He was on his second tour in Viet Nam, and wanted a third; he was a bachelor. He was an Advisor for the Popular Forces (PF), a volunteer local militia force.

He thought that, for the money spent, they were the best fighting forces in Viet Nam. They were poorly informed, poorly equipped, and not well trained, but they volunteered to serve as military men in their own home areas.

To illustrate how poorly informed they were, one man could not name his district chief or the Province Chief, and thought that the head of the South Vietnamese government was Ho Chi Minh. But he had joined the PF to kill VC. Perhaps if he wanted to kill VC for Ho Chi Minh (boss of the VC), General Ky and even his district chief would accept his efforts.

The PF did not operate in big units, so they did not have any big fights, but they constantly harassed and ambushed the VC. Not long before, for instance, a platoon of PF had ambushed a VC Company (three times as big a force), and killed or captured 37, without having any of their own even scratched.

Johnson wasn't the only one who wanted to stay. I heard about an ALO, a bachelor also, who had kept volunteering and was on his third tour in country.

We had several Jeeps for our operation, but they had gotten into such bad shape they would hardly run. I finally found the US Army Detachment that was supposed to maintain them, so, one at a time, we at last got all of them to running pretty well.

I spent most of Day 119 (Saturday, November 5), writing an After Action Report on Operation Irving. Essentially it said that Operation Irving was a big success. It had just about eliminated several VC battalions, cleared the VC from an area where they had operated for a long time, and killed or captured more than 4,000. (We didn't keep a body count. Captured was better than killed, anyway.) And I couldn't take credit for any of it. All I did was fly over the action a little bit, and sit in a tent watching the rain come down.

Clarence Rustvold, my senior FAC at Cheo Reo, left for home on Emergency Leave that day. His father had died. Darryl Dixon was now my only FAC there. We did get a new FAC. More were supposed to be on the way.

On Sunday I took an O-1 to Pleiku for a 50-hour Inspection, but had to stay overnight for a carburetor change. It was so cold I ended up sleeping under two blankets.

In my days in SAC, I frequently piloted Radar Bomb Scored (RBS) training missions. We would be given the exact coordinates of a selected target, with nearby points which would provide good radar returns. These points were used as radar offsets for the primary target. Departing from a designated Initial Point, we would make a simulated bombing run on the target, using the airplane's bombing/navigation system. A radar crew on the ground would track us, and we'd transmit a tone on the radio. The bomb release system would interrupt the tone at the bomb release point, so that the ground radar crew had a fix on us at that precise point. Using our ground speed and heading and the ballistics of the presumed weapon, the ground crew could then predict the point at which the bomb would have hit, and give us a score accordingly.

Now the same system and crews were directing bomb runs in Viet Nam. I watched the operation one night in Pleiku. They were directing F-100's in an attack on Viet Cong forces who were assaulting a Special Forces camp, steering a flight of four F-100's down the bomb run and telling them when to salvo their bombs. The friendlies on the ground could tell them, by radio, where the bombs actually hit. I had always had an adversarial relationship with RBS, but here they were on our side.

Another "Care" package came from home; Mama-san thought the chocolate chip cookies were Number 1.

There was eight inches of snow in Ohio; just rain in VN.

In honor of Bill Coon's imminent departure, we went out for a genuine Chinese dinner "on the economy". It was the same kind of Chinese as back home, sweet and sour several things, fried rice, red Algerian wine with the meal, hot tea, then warm wet wash cloths at the end--total cost for me was 350 P, a real bargain, I thought.

Bill got on his way home on Thursday morning. He was to meet his wife in Las Vegas. He said he was feeling quite nervous, like he was about to go on a honeymoon or something.

On Saturday evening there was another "Hail and Farewell" party, to welcome newcomers and say goodbye to those about to leave. It was attended by most of the Advisors of Group 22, and by 15 or 20 Vietnamese Officers. Col. Hieu, Lt. Col. Hung, Lt. Col. Vong and one other VN Officer brought their wives. The ladies wore colorful but traditional ao dais. All the men wore sport shirts, except Col. Vong, who wore a summer suit.

There were speeches by Col. Hunter, Senior Advisor, Lt. Col. Stephens, his deputy, and Col. Hieu. I thought Hieu's talk was the best.

I met Major Chima of the Indian Army. He was a member of the International Control Commission, which was supposed to be seeing that the agreements made at Geneva in 1954 concerning Viet Nam were being kept. I also knew Major Purser, the Canadian member. I hadn't met the Polish member of the team. Major Chima was at least six feet-four, always wore his beard tied up in a certain way, and a blue turban, in or out of uniform. He was a Sikh, I guessed, though I didn't ask him.

While at Pleiku on Sunday, November 13, I drove a Jeep with a bit of a history. An Airman at Pleiku had a Vietnamese girl friend at Bien Hoa, and decided to drive this particular Jeep there to see her, through a couple hundred miles of VC territory. Somewhere down the road he ran out of gas. The ARVN found the Jeep and retrieved it. But the VC got the Airman, and still had him. He had two problems, he was AWOL from the US Air Force, subject to Court Martial, and he was a prisoner of the enemy. Was the chance of seeing a girl friend worth it?

We had a problem closer to home. One of our airmen, an airplane mechanic, was married, with three children at home and another on the way, but couldn't do without sex for more than four or five days. Vietnamese girls were available, and he found one who kept him in cigarettes, furnished him a room, and also gave him gonorrhea. The Medics could cure that, but he was violating the curfew on US forces, getting himself in a jam, and his superiors in trouble for not being able to maintain discipline. While he was always on the job when he was supposed to be, and did good work, he was causing his Sergeant gray hairs and sleepless nights. The Sergeant's only recourse was to "bust" him, but the reduction in pay would work a hardship on his family instead of on him.

I read with great interest the Classified (Confidential) report of Navy Lt. Dieter Dengler, who was shot down over North Viet Nam, was captured and imprisoned, escaped, and evaded successfully. He was spotted from the air by Lt. Col. Dietrick from Pleiku, whom I knew. Dietrick called in a helicopter to pick him up. He weighed only about 98 pounds when he was rescued. I doubted that I could have survived all that he did.

Our airman further muddied the waters by going through the Vietnamese formula for marriage to a woman with two children. More complications were to be expected. What if his real wife back in the States were to hear about it?

I was still more dismayed about published news reports in US print media concerning our operations and the fighting going on in Viet Nam. If all the reporting was as inaccurate and downright false as what I had read, the US public was being completely misled. Time magazine made Operation Irving sound like an accidental, spur of the moment thing, begun when a First Cavalry helicopter was shot down. The article completely left out any account of all the planning that went into the operation, and hardly mentioned the parts played by the Vietnamese 22nd ARVN and 3rd Airborne troops, the ROK Capital Division and other units. Not mentioned at all was the large number of prisoners taken, a new record in the war. The article said the VC had not attacked in battalion strength that year. In fact they and/or the NVA had attacked twice in multi battalion strength in Binh Dinh Province in September alone. The news reporting was one sided, inaccurate, and completely missed very significant happenings.

A well known newspaper columnist came bursting into our Operations one day, demanding to be shown the camp where captured Viet Cong and North Vietnamese Army men were being tortured. Of course no such place existed. Where did they get such outlandish information?

At breakfast on Sunday morning I talked to US Army Captain Nixon. He was an Advisor to the 22nd ARVN Reconnaissance Company, and was the man I talked to on the radio whenever I flew air cover for the unit in the field. His wife was a Home Economics student at Kansas State, in Manhattan. Our support was much appreciated. Their appreciation for us was much appreciated, too. Besides, they were helpful to us.

I tried talking French to Mama-san, but it didn't work. She thought I was talking about church, and assured me she had already been that morning. She probably thought I was talking about Church because most of the nuns and priests she knew spoke at least some French.

One had to pay attention to the gestures he used in dealing with the Vietnamese. One evening I was stopped for traffic in my Jeep, when I saw several Vietnamese Catholic Nuns along the street. Wanting to be friendly, I stuck out my hand, palm down, to wave to them. To Vietnamese, I discovered (or was reminded) that that meant,

"Come and join me!"

So they did, about six of them, chattering and laughing and having a good time. The one beside me gave me directions with hand signals until we arrived at their house. They all piled out, expressing their thanks in Vietnamese, even in French and English.

CHAPTER XI

MORE HELP ARRIVES

Two days before Thanksgiving, Major Bob Smith checked in as our latest FAC, and three more were supposed to be on the way. That would give me a total of 14, three each at Tuy Hoa and Cheo Reo and a total of eight of us at Qui Nhon. That would severely crowd our living quarters.

I would have to begin some very careful balancing in assignments, so as not to have juniors in charge of seniors. It had never been a personal problem for me, because it was quite common in SAC for a Captain Aircraft Commander to have Lt. Colonels assigned as Navigators or Radar Operators on his crew. One of our men was not going to be a problem, Jack Moore was on the list of new Lt. Colonels. He was TDY, so I didn't get to congratulate him right away.

It was kind of difficult to get around to letter writing. Right after supper we would all meet to be briefed by our Intelligence Clerk, Airman Liley, on the newest events and information of the day. We'd review new VR sightings, and results of fighter strikes. The Line Chief, M/Sgt. Keim, would come by and we'd discuss airplane problems and maintenance personnel concerns. Then I'd have to try to catch up on official correspondence of the day and Administrative matters. I was continually interrupted by people stopping in on business, semi-business or social calls. When everyone else got tired out and went to bed, I could finally write letters.

Thanksgiving Day was another work day, making the rounds to Pleiku, Cheo Reo and Tuy Hoa. I had Thanksgiving dinner at Pleiku and again at Qui Nhon. It was the same at both places--turkey, etc.

Another airman had troubles. They become the commander's troubles, too. He came in after dinner on Thanksgiving evening to tell me his wife of seven months had disappeared. She had been staying with his parents, who lived only a few blocks from her own parents, and working in a small factory. He was afraid she would harm herself in the mood she was in when she left, with a tendency to drive into walls, poles, ditches, etc. Her parents didn't know where she had gone, either. She was depressed, taking doctor prescribed tranquilizers for extreme nervousness, and frequently became very emotional. Partly she was depressed because she hadn't been able to get pregnant before he left for Viet Nam.

His father had inquired at where she worked, but was told she had been fired for absenteeism. The airman was afraid she wouldn't have any money to live on, since his allotment hadn't been coming yet. And she hadn't been stopping by his parents' house to pick up her mail, as she had said she would.

The letter from his father was nine days old, so we decided to try getting in touch through MARS, if that didn't work, we'd go to the Red Cross first thing in the morning.

We had been threatened with a typhoon Thanksgiving evening, it even had a name, Nancy. But the winds around it slowed down, and it was downgraded to a tropical disturbance. It brought lots of heavy rain, with a possibility of winds up to fifty miles per hour, to last for up to 48 hours. We had all our airplanes securely tied down, with sand bags on their horizontal tails, so we didn't worry about them. Our only concern was that the VC might attack some time during the night, and we would not be able to go and help because of the weather.

I was finally getting the operation organized the way I thought it should be. When I first arrived, it was sort of a "fly your heads off" kind of thing because of so many targets and so few people to direct strikes. Now we could spend a lot more time in our liaison jobs, and I could assign a specific FAC to each organization needing our support, which I hoped would make us more effective. Also, I understood the whole job a lot better than at the beginning, and had been able to establish good rapport with those we supported. That gave me a sense of accomplishment.

I made a sort of formal call on Trung-ta (Lt. Col.) Vong, the Province Chief of Binh Dinh, and, over tea, explained our FAC assignment program, and who would provide assistance to his units, such as the Regional and Provincial Armed Forces under his command. He was cordial and appreciative. The tea was good, too.

News from Wright-Patterson--one of my old bosses had been returned to the cockpit, and departed for A-1E training in mid-November. Perhaps he would get assigned to Pleiku and put in fighter strikes for us. Another long time friend asked if I had yet visited the Leprosarium just down the coast from Qui Nhon. Her brother, Msgr. Feiten, had visited there and at Kontum with his Bishop, the year before. Her extended family had made up a purse for the Leprosarium and another for the Diocese of Kontum, instead of exchanging gifts among themselves, the previous Christmas. I put the Leprosarium on my list of places to visit when I could find time.

We were blessed with another new FAC, Capt. Phil Jones. Now we were feeling a pinch in the motor transportation department, and needed another Jeep! Not just for him, of course.

We got some help in that department when the 22nd ARVN assigned me a Japanese built (Toyota) Jeep style vehicle. It rode quite a bit rougher than the swing-axle Ford, but the Vietnamese maintenance crew took good care of it. It always hit on all four cylinders, and they took it in once a week when I wasn't using it, for cleaning and any necessary or scheduled maintenance.

On Sunday, November 27, Day 141, we were finally able to get one flight up; it didn't get very far.

The airman with the missing wife finally got a call through to his father. She was still missing, hadn't come by to pick up her mail, and it contained allotment checks which she was to use to pay their bills. She had left the payment books with his parents, but of course they couldn't cash the allotment checks. He was afraid she might be staying with her older sister, who was herself rather unstable. We really couldn't afford to have a man working on airplanes who couldn't keep his mind on his work, so I began exploring the possibility of an Emergency Leave for him to go see if he could find her and perhaps get things straightened out.

On Monday after Thanksgiving I was finally able to get up and fly for an hour with Phil Jones in the back seat. I discovered that evening, while practicing on the guitar to lead " Come, Oh Come, Emmanuel" for church the next Sunday, that Phil was also Catholic.

I asked for two more rooms for FAC's. I'd be lucky to get one. We now had seven men and an Office in two rooms; the shared bathroom was overloaded. The whole compound was overcrowded. At least some of the nurses were supposed to move to quarters adjacent to the hospital, but no one knew when that would be.

With all the rain we'd had, the valley West and Northwest of Qui Nhon had become one big lake. I had to revise my estimate that the individual hamlets were on sufficiently higher ground to avoid flooding. Most of them now had six inches to a foot of water in them.

Qui Nhon, with all the rain and heavy trucks, had become a quagmire. Two of the main streets had been closed in order to repair them. The detours had been reduced to series of mud and water holes. On the side streets there were no side walks, and the first floors were at street level, so mud and water splashed across the narrow front yards and into the front doors of houses and hovels alike.

The residents couldn't walk anywhere without getting into the mud. The poor girls in their pretty ao dais couldn't avoid getting splattered with mud from vehicles driven by totally inconsiderate drivers, who had no concern for them. I tried very hard not to splatter anyone, or make anyone jump into the deep slop. There were two basic problems, drainage was totally inadequate, and the trucks had to do their work.

Bill Owen, whom I knew, was flying A-1's out of Pleiku.

Figure 11.1
Flooding in the Rural Areas

Figure 11.2
Flooded Hamlets

He had a severe back problem. The Flight Surgeon met him at his airplane one day and shipped him straight to the Clark Field Hospital. There he had a myelogram, and a spinal disc removed. They didn't even fuse any vertebrae. He was back in the air three weeks after the operation! Keep 'em flying!

We didn't fly at all on Thursday (December 1), because of high winds. Had the temperature been 40 degrees cooler, we'd have been having a howling blizzard, the rain was coming down in sheets.

Our problem airman (the wandering one) was notified that his stepfather had died. His wife and his mother requested that he be given Emergency Leave. The expected baby might arrive while he was there. Perhaps that would help him straighten up.

I had a successful trip to Pleiku on Tuesday, getting other business done besides an airplane inspection. The weather was pretty poor over the hills, so my route was mostly around them.

The O-1 was surely not an executive's type airplane, but it served well at getting around to the places I had to go. I was getting spoiled, for sure, an executive with a company airplane to fly.

On my return from Pleiku, I was flying in light rain with the sun shining low behind me. Real magic happened as I was coasting down from the Highlands, passing An Khe. Ahead of me suddenly appeared the complete circle of a beautiful rainbow, except that I couldn't see it directly under the airplane's nose. It was as if the airplane and I were wearing a huge halo. No wonder I loved to fly.

The evening of December 8, we had a thirty minute show by Martha Raye. She told some jokes, sang some songs, and made faces as only she could make them. I supposed she got paid for those trips, but they must still have been pretty rough. She was surely no glamour girl, and was old enough to be the mother of most of the younger Army and Air Force men and women she entertained, but they loved her and appreciated the effort she made to bring in a few rays of sunshine. She must have loved them, too. After the show she visited with the young people and freely dispensed hugs.

Clarence Rustvold returned from his emergency leave the next day. He said it was mighty cold in Minnesota. We'd been hearing about big snowstorms in the USA.

I started over to Cheo Reo to pick up Gordon Beck, who had been substituting for Clarence.

The trip across the hills and jungle to Cheo Reo was always interesting and challenging. It was inhabited, if at all, by unfriendlies. I had heard shots, some .50 caliber or larger, fired at me on several occasions. The route started up a wide valley past the ROK flight strip, then past a Green Beret camp with a genuine Goodyear rubber runway. Then it crossed several low ridges and climbed to higher terrain out over the real jungle.

On this particular morning, I had passed the Green Beret strip and was several miles into my climb over the higher terrain when the engine suddenly almost quit completely. There was nothing but jungle beneath me. My heart did about four fast flip-flops, as I did a quick reversal of direction, back toward the air strip, reducing to best glide speed.

Desperately working the mixture control, the carburetor heat control, the throttle, the fuel tank selector and the ignition switch, I got the engine running roughly, and headed back toward Qui Nhon, by way of the air strips and flat ground. When I got back, the mechanics changed three spark plugs.

The engine checked out, so I headed out to Cheo Reo again to pick up Gordon. Before we started back, Cheo Reo's mechanics changed one of the new plugs our men had just put in. About 15 minutes into the trip back, the engine began running rough again. I nursed it along and we finally arrived safely back at home base. The mechanics worked on it for several hours. I thought it might need a cylinder change.

Fouling spark plugs and burned valves resulted from one thing. The US Armed Forces had been directed by Mr. Robert S.

121

McNamara to buy only one grade of aviation gasoline. Because the big, powerful engines had to have highly leaded, high octane fuel, 115/145, to avoid detonation, that was the kind we got, too. The problem with the O-1's little engine was that it couldn't digest all that lead. The spark plugs fouled with lead deposits, and too much lead also burned the valves. The engine, in civilian use, with 87 octane fuel, ran 1700 hours between overhauls. We couldn't get more than 750. I was tempted to wonder how many of our small aircraft were shot down by our own fuel.

The weather turned out fine on Friday. I made the quickest round trip yet to Pleiku. It included an airplane inspection, pick up of some radio parts, some calamine lotion from the Air Force Dispensary, and emergency requisition of two pairs of heavy socks from Clothing Sales. I got back so quickly that I surprised both myself and the maintenance people.

A friend stationed at Andrews AFB wrote that AFSC had requested me by name for my next assignment. His wife, my wife's very dear friend, hoped I'd be assigned to Andrews.

I flew a regular mission on Sunday, then on down to Nha Trang, home of the 21st Tactical Air Support Squadron, to whom all the FAC's in II Corps belonged. I entered my formal request for next assignment to ASD/AFSC at Wright-Patterson, where my family was.

Another quick trip to Tuy Hoa to deliver an airplane, on Thursday, the 15th--Jack Henry flew on my wing going down. We hardly ever flew formation! I rode in the back seat with him on the way back.

Flying Friday morning was not very successful, I took off at 0650 and got :20, again at 0845 and got 1:10. There was a big row of thunderstorms across my planned path.

Friday evening, December 16, there was another special event at the ARVN Officers Club, a farewell party for Col. Hunter, the US Army Senior Advisor, with two generals present, Meyer from Qui Nhon and Lee from Pleiku. As usual, the best speech, in English, was by Col. Hieu. Had all the Vietnamese leaders been as competent as he was, they'd have needed a lot less help.

On Saturday morning, I was flying North of the Bong

Figure 11.3
Herb 01 Ready to Go Fly

Figure 11.4
Herb 01 Back from a Mission, Looks a Little Beaten

Son, near English Air Field, when I got a call from an Army O-1 pilot, a "Head Hunter" whom I knew, Capt. John Philbrick. The area was covered by a layer of low clouds, which thinned out to broken clouds to the North. He reported that he had been fired at, in the Northern part of the area, just inside the Northern border of Binh Dinh Province, and had some battle damage. A bullet tore through his airplane, ruined an instrument, and cut the fuel line to his fuel pressure gauge, causing fuel to leak into the cockpit. The bullet made neat holes in the airplane skin, the floor and a rudder pedal, and rough ones in the instrument cowling and the windshield.

He asked me to help him get lined up to descend through the clouds to land. I located him, then, using the surrounding hill tops showing above the clouds as guides, steered him for a safe descent to English. Presently he reported under the clouds with the field in sight, and finally reported safely on the ground. I flew to the area where he had reported the fire coming from, but couldn't see anything, and was not shot at. I concluded he had been flying lower than I recommended for our FAC's, and presented too good a target for the VC rifleman to ignore.

I went back to English and landed after the clouds overhead had thinned a bit. I got a list of parts to make the airplane flyable, which I took back to the Head Hunter outfit at Qui Nhon. They sent the parts and a mechanic to English, and had the airplane back that afternoon.

An interesting sidelight to the episode was that Philbrick had just returned from a month in an Army Hospital in Japan, recovering from a wound in his heel, inflicted by a rifle round fired at him from the ground.

That day completed my 23rd week outside the USA.

Every so often I'd get a hair cut at the BX sponsored barber shop. The price was about 20 P. I always tipped the barber an equal amount.

Another amazing use for scissors--in the few places there was grass to be trimmed, the tool used was a big pair of scissors.

CHAPTER XII

THE HOLIDAYS

On Tuesday, the 20th, Jack Henry and I flew to Pleiku, and spent several hours talking with our counterparts at II DASC.

The talks dealt with direct air support in the II Corps area. We found out we'd be flying during the Holiday truces, but not directing any air strikes, just looking.

Much of our discussion centered around communications problems, and trying to devise means of solving them. Part of the problems were due to poor radio and telephone equipment, part due to language differences, and part due to differences in thinking processes and basic philosophy. All those things were what made my Liaison job so important, getting everyone to working together. It had seemed to be working when I arrived in August, but when I finally had the time and the manpower to begin doing the job right, I found out that it hadn't really been getting done.

Now I was trying to get everything ironed out. I decided that I must devise a kind of job description for the ALO who would follow me, telling how to accomplish the mission, whom else to deal with, and so on. I had found that approach useful in both SAC and ASD.

That evening the Senior Catholic Chaplain in the Qui Nhon area, Father (Lt. Col.) Miller, dropped in to ask if I would do the readings from the Old Testament and the Epistle during Cardinal Spellman's Mass on Christmas Day. Of course I accepted the assignment.

Bad news from a few days earlier: A convoy was on the way, from Cheo Reo to Pleiku, to pick up the goodies for Christmas Dinner, when it was attacked by the VC. One American and a number of Vietnamese were killed. One Vietnamese woman saw her husband and her child killed. She grabbed a gun and started shooting at the VC, killing about three of them, The others shot her and stabbed her several times with bayonets. She was rescued and taken to the hospital at Cheo Reo, where she was recovering from her wounds. I thought she should be awarded some kind of heroine's medal, but that, of course, wouldn't bring her family back. What a terrible thing to happen just before Christmas. Truly the Vietnamese people needed our prayers.

Thursday, the 22nd, brought another successful round trip to Pleiku, and it was only 2:05 flying time.

Friday arrived with more rain, and more troubles. At dinner that evening, Lt. Col. Rupple, Senior Army Advisor, told me there was more serious flooding out in the valley, and helicopters had spent most of the afternoon rescuing flood victims from some of the hamlets. He said about 25 children were missing, or separated from their parents. He was afraid that at least some of them had drowned.

A Vietnamese woman who worked for the Mess Association wrote a short letter of appreciation for all the American Mess members, and made copies for all of us. I thought her English was quite good. We all felt genuinely appreciated. In part she wrote,

"--You are here because of us. You are now living far from your country and your families to help us gain and guard the freedom and peace so that we have a future.

" The Vietnamese people and I do not know how else to express our appreciation and gratefulness to you except to say 'God Bless You' and many thanks because many Americans are sacrificing their lives for my country. Respectfully, MISS TAM

" Miss Tam for the Vietnamese People".

The weather did not seem very Christmas-y, but there were Christmas decorations up in the Mess, the Club, and all the work places.

A nice Christmas present: Gordon Beck was on the list of those selected to become Majors.

Good friends had sent me a small *Creche* (Nativity Scene), which I set up on my desk. St. Joseph was holding a lantern, all the other figures were pretty conventional. Mama-san saw it and was fascinated. She spent many minutes studying it, and pronounced it Number 1. I had the thought that there are many wonderful people in the world, and Viet Nam had at least its share of them.

We were supposed to fly surveillance on December 24, but the weather shut us out completely.

When I went to the Christmas Eve Party at the Club, there was a huge crowd in the streets, concentrated at and near the Catholic Cathedral. The curfew precluded my going to Midnight Mass there, and really kind of inhibited going across town to the Qui Nhon Service Command Chapel. Phil Jones and I went anyway. It was jammed, as I expected. At the last minute I found myself the Lector (Reader) and leader of the singing. Very helpfully, we had an organist. We sang " O Come, All Ye Faithful", "Joy to the World", and " Silent Night". It was easy and enjoyable.

Christmas Day was on Sunday, and turned out clear, sparkling and beautiful, like a late Spring day right after rain in the Midwestern United States. I flew about 1:30 that morning, just looking, of course.

Cardinal Spellman's Mass was in the afternoon, in a large hangar on the flight line. It was filled. He was pretty feeble, and, since I was already on the platform to do the Readings, I helped him to his chair.

When Sermon time came, he gave a nice talk, the gist of which was that he was very pleased with the efforts of American Servicemen, missionaries, and others, and those people from other nations, to bring peace to the world. Of course, he was speaking as an American citizen, not as a spokesman for the Catholic Church. He also thanked everyone who had helped with the arrangements and with the Mass that afternoon.

The Cardinal was the Military Ordinary of the United States, which meant he was the Bishop for Catholics of all the US Armed Forces.

Christmas Dinner was good, but not the same as home cooking. It had been a memorable day, the best I could ever hope for so far away from my family.

One of the activities that went on in the Qui Nhon area was a sortie, or expedition, mission, or something, that went out about one day a week from the US Army Hospital. A team of one or more Doctors, several Medical Corpsmen, and Nurses, would go out to a hamlet or two within reasonable driving distance, and provide Sick Call for the residents. They could fix minor ills, hand out standard pills, and provide treatment for injuries, for the children, women and men who got no other medical care. I personally felt great pride in our people, and gratitude for the country of which I was privileged to be a part.

The day after Christmas, Bob Hope and his troupe came to entertain us. I did plan to go, but after considering the discomforts of sitting or standing for hours on the hard pavement, decided to stay near the radio room in sort of an alert status. Jack Moore and three of our other pilots went. After the show was already 45 minutes late, Jack gave up and came back. Those who stayed said it finally got started about an hour late, and they enjoyed it.

I scheduled John Welch to take the 27th off.

My day off began the next morning with being awakened at 0415 by a report of a mortar attack on Hoai An, the same outpost I'd lost sleep over two or three times before. I got Major Love airborne at 0450, with an AC-47 on the way from Pleiku. I found out later that the last mortar round burst at 0400. The VC probably picked up their mortar tubes and headed back to their camp by 0405. Spooky got there and dropped flares, but neither its crew, nor the FAC, nor the troops on the ground, got any visual or other contact. Anyway, no one was hurt. I got back in bed at 0545, and stayed there until 0930. I loafed as much as I could, I wasn't scheduled to fly, but got involved in business just the same. So much for a " day off".

The next day, I got word of a move to transfer Curt Love and Jack Moore away from us. On Thursday I went to Pleiku to see what was going on. Sure enough, Curt was going to Dalat, and Jack to Ban Me Thuot.

I could tell I was " getting the old business" as soon as I saw Lt. Col. Scroggin, my boss. His first word was "Hello". The next words were,

" You've been doing an outstanding job down there at Qui Nhon."

Dalat was considered the resort spot of South Viet Nam, so Curt was going to a good place, even though he didn't want to leave Qui Nhon. Jack was going to Ban Me Thuot to fill the same position he held with us, Division FAC. He'd be working for Col. Norman Mueller, whom I knew at Wright-Patt, and who went through the training at Hurlburt with me. Scroggin said Norm needed a good right hand man, which Jack certainly would be. I was to get Major Dave Griffin, a brand new man, whenever he showed up. He had been a Major since 1960, so probably had been passed over for promotion at least once or twice. Scroggin just about admitted that I was considered as running a training program.

I would be losing Jack Henry when he returned to the States in January. I had planned to move Curt Love into Jack's position when he left. No one is indispensable; I'd get someone trained into his slot.

Our landing skills were tested that day, strong gusty crosswinds, but we " overcame".

Friday developed into an interesting and busy day. With Capt. Rex Miller, our newest FAC, in the back seat, I took off at 0610 and put in two air strikes. That afternoon, one of my FAC's at Tuy Hoa, with a passenger on board, crashed in the shallow water of Song Cau Bay, South of Qui Nhon. The airplane was demolished, but they didn't seem badly hurt. I saw them briefly at the receiving room at the hospital. They looked rather pale, with minor cuts and bruises. I was saddened by the loss of the airplane, but I was further saddened by what I thought might have happened. It seemed possible that Paul was doing some maneuvers he shouldn't have, and knew better than to do. When I asked if the engine had quit, he replied,

" No, sir, I did a foolish thing."

He told one of the other pilots he stalled in. He said later that he tried to do a slow roll. I heard descriptions of the accident by two eye-witnesses, the 22nd Division Senior Advisor and his Deputy. They said the airplane was never inverted.

They landed in about two feet of water, and men on the shore waded out to help them out of the airplane and to dry land.

Oh, well, another of a commander's typical woes.

And Rex Miller filled our eighth bed. We didn't even have a place for him to hang his clothes. We'd have to wait until the two men left the next week.

Here it was, the last day of 1966, and it was a busy one, too. Because of the accident the day before, Col. Sansing, O-1 Squadron Commander, and Col. Strain, Deputy Commander of the 504th Support Group, came from Danang. Col. Ransbottom, my Squadron Commander, and Maj. Dale came from Nha Trang, and Joe Wratten came from Tuy Hoa. Maj. William C. Dale was to be the Accident Investigation Officer. Dale told me he had worked just down the hall from me at Wright-Patterson, in famous Building 125.

They were all lucky to get in. The weather was so bad all day long that we got only one twenty minute FAC flight. The visitors all managed to sneak in and out along the coast during brief letups in the rain and heavy clouds. Capt. Paul Parton and his passenger in the accident, Navy Lt. Paul Aquilino, were in pretty good physical condition, though sore.

Paul Parton felt pretty bad about the accident, he was no doubt concerned that he might have to meet a Flying Evaluation Board, which might end his military flying career. And he might not be able to go and meet his wife on R & R in Hawaii for five days, scheduled for January 13. He said the accident happened when he did a slow or barrel roll, and stalled out from it. He knew acrobatics was prohibited in the O-1, which was why he was so worried about it,

All of us FAC's were invited to the Province Chief's (Lt. Col. Vong's) New Year's Eve Party. It was formal, which we found out meant with coat and tie. I dug my summer suit out of the closet. I could have stayed in the room to write letters, but decided I owed Col. Vong the courtesy of attending his party, to be held at the ARVN Officers Club just two blocks up the street.

The party turned out to be the most elaborate I had ever attended. We arrived about 9:30, and young Vietnamese lads and lasses met us at the door, found our name tags, pinned them on, and conducted us to the bars, where beer and mixed drinks were being served. Half an hour later, we were asked to move to the ballroom and take seats. An orchestra had been playing, and now the curtain at the end of the room opened and two high school girls and two high school boys sang patriotic Vietnamese songs. One of the girls was quite small, and wore a little girl style dress.

At the end of their songs, the orchestra struck up dance music, and the Vongs led off the dancing. Col. Vong wore a white mess dress, and Madame Vong wore a pretty ao dai, white satin trousers and a peach colored outer garment. There were quite a few Vietnamese ladies, mostly in colorful ao dais, but some younger ones wore modern Western dresses. The two Korean ladies wore very high waisted gowns with very bouffant skirts.

I danced once, a waltz with Madame Vong. She spoke a little English, I no Vietnamese. She was very gracious when I stepped on the edge of her shoe a couple of times.

After a series of dancing selections, the curtain opened again to reveal--The Rolling Five--long hair, striped shirts, "Yea! Yea!" and all. NOISY!?! Two guitars, a four stringed instrument I didn't recognize, all with amplifiers, drums and a tambourine. Rock and Roll was everywhere! Well, perhaps not in Hanoi. But these guys were as good as the Beatles, the Rolling Stones or Herman's Hermits. They sang some songs, even some in English, did a couple of instrumentals, and played some dance numbers.

Then came the show of the evening, a history of the ao dai from its earliest days hundreds of years ago. The models were from the Normal (teacher training) School, obviously with no training as models, but so pretty, sweet and shy they were completely charming.

Then the little high school girl came back and sang a beautiful Vietnamese song. She was quite good, with a better microphone presence than many professionals I had seen. A young man sang a solo, then the Rolling Five did a couple more numbers.

On the stroke of midnight, the stage curtain opened and Col. Vong came out on the stage with a Vietnamese girl, one of the Korean ladies, and our own USO girl, Pat Kelley. He wished us Happy New Year in Vietnamese, English and Korean. He then introduced each girl in her own language, and each unfurled a small banner, representative of her country. After that the three paraded down the aisle and back, tossing fresh strawberries into the audience on either side. What was the significance of that? I didn't know!

Not long afterward, a buffet lunch was served in the garden (between the Club front entrance and the beach). So I welcomed in the New Year, 1967, out in the open under occasional stars, listening to the surf on the beach, eating a vegetable salad and macaroni with a meat sauce. I listened to the music a while longer, and at about 1:15 paid my respects to the Vongs, wishing them a Western Happy New Year (Tet was yet to come), and walked back to Quarters. And soon the rain came down.

CHAPTER XIII

1967 WAS HERE!

The rain stayed with us, and I scheduled me to take the day off on January 2, 1967. The weather was so bad we couldn't fly anyway. It was just as well, I had the flu or something so bad that I ached all over, inside and out. I finally was up to eating dinner on Tuesday evening.

Wednesday continued the wet, cool (about 70 degrees) weather, with heavy cloud cover, precluding any flying. I didn't hear of any VC activity, either.

Many of the Vietnamese managed to find sweaters somewhere, and even pants for most of the usually pantsless ones.

The nature and cause of Parton's accident continued a bit elusive. Paul said he rolled the airplane, witnesses said it didn't roll, some said the engine quit. The Accident Investigation Officer asked the Flight Surgeon at Tuy Hoa to come and talk to Paul; he suspected Paul was trying to use the accident to get removed from flying status.

Curt Love's little boy sent him some soft plastic "creepy crawlies" for Christmas, two lizards and a big, black spider. Curt put the spider on the back of Mama-san's hand. She looked at it, fascinated, for a moment, then ran out to try to scare some of the other maids with it.

I had been observing that people everywhere are a lot alike. Favorite play activities of the Vietnamese children included skipping and jumping rope, playing hop scotch, shooting marbles and spinning tops.

Jack Moore was delaying my taking him to Ban Me Thuot, waiting for his R and R orders to go spend five days in Hawaii with his wife. The orders came on Thursday. It was the first time I had seen him so excited about anything. Obviously he still loved his wife. The weather cooperated, and I flew him to his new assignment on Friday. That airplane was pretty well loaded, with the two of us and all his gear.

Alberta sent me a pack of Christmas Cards from relatives and friends. They all said they were praying for me, ranging from very formal commitments to RB-36 Crewmate Pappy Wayne's noting what he called his wife Dorothy's "incantations". With so many prayers, some benefit must have come, good health and safety, or sainthood. That last seemed highly unlikely. If all those people had stopped praying for me, I'd probably have collapsed in a useless heap.

Jack Henry got word of his next assignment, he'd be going to the 2750th Air Base Wing, at Wright-Patterson, as an instructor pilot. He'd be leaving us the second week in January. Curt Love was due at Dalat on January 15. With that, I'd have lost my three most experienced FAC's. Rex Miller was now fully checked out. Maj. Griffin was due in just any day, to replace Maj. Moore.

Worth noting--Saturday was my 182nd day into my tour. Midnight was exactly half way through my " sentence". All down hill from there on?

Also on Saturday, Housing assigned us another room, specifically for three captains. It had been occupied by about four sergeants. We couldn't move anyone in yet; there was no furniture, and no lights, and the walls were in serious need of paint.

Dave Griffin arrived on Sunday. His last assignment had been flying C-124's, an airplane I'd considered volunteering for more than a year earlier.

Tuesday took me to Pleiku. Among other things, Scroggin wanted some notes on what I'd been doing. He was slated to leave his position to return to the States in February, and had to prepare an OER (Officer Effectiveness Report) for me for the time he'd been my boss. He gave my ego a boost when he told me he considered my work as an ALO to be outstanding, the best in II Corps. He said he was writing an EWQ (Exceptionally Well Qualified) (Outstanding) report on me. I supposed that would help if I ever came up for consideration for promotion, unlikely since I was a Reserve Officer instead of Regular.

Gordon Beck, one of my FAC's, came in to visit me for about two hours in the evening. He talked about his ambition to go from his FAC assignment back to the Training Command to teach flying to flight students.

Jack Henry left for the States, and Curt Love to Dalat, leaving me with five FAC's at Qui Nhon, only three of whom had any experience in the job. Yes, we were in the training business.

I had begun really liking my assignment. Had I been a bachelor, I would probably have volunteered for another year in the same position. There were inconveniences, but I wasn't physically hurting. The job was rewarding, the people I worked with were capable and dedicated to their mission, and I believed we were doing something very worthwhile for the people of Viet Nam.

The weather got so cool that Mama-san, knowing I didn't have a blanket, got out my second mattress cover and put it at the foot of my bed. Motherly, I thought.

I continued making improvements in the ALO operation. By the time we ran out of a job (no more VC), we'd know how to do it.

Nothing disastrous happened on Friday, the 13th!

On Sunday evening, January 15 (Day 190, 175 to go), I got a request from Saigon to nominate a volunteer to Ton Son Nhut, to become a briefing officer to talk to Big Shots and newcomers to the Theater, on the subject of Tactical Air Support. Dave Griffin volunteered, but didn't have any experience to talk from, Paul Parton was set for R and R, and I couldn't reach Darryl Dixon. I was eligible but didn't think I'd like to leave the 22nd in the lurch. So, I didn't nominate anyone.

We went to the Club to bid an Army Captain goodbye. His wife was a student in Home Economics at Kansas State University, my old Alma Mater. He expected to arrive there on January 19, and she had a big Final Exam on January 20!!

The weather continued cold, wet and windy, no flying, expecting no change through Wednesday. Mama-san decided to spread the wealth around, so she got my extra mattress cover out and put it on Phil Jones' bed. He thought it was great.

Paul Parton and his passenger in the accident got out of the hospital, and Paul went to join his wife in Hawaii. There was not so far any determination of the cause of the accident. Witnesses did not see the airplane inverted, so if he <u>tried</u> to roll he might just have gotten into an unusual position and lost it in recovery.

One trouble I had trying to write letters was that I maintained an open door policy with the men working for me. It was a rare evening that someone didn't come and sit down to talk for an hour or so. For instance, M/Sgt. Keim, my Maintenance Chief, came in to discuss some of his problems with some of the men, and, getting his "9-level" AFSC (Air Force Specialty Code). The 9-level (9 as the last number of his AFSC) is the highest qualification in enlisted specialties, and means the man is qualified as a top level supervisor. It also gives him better assignment opportunities, and a chance to be promoted to Senior Master Sergeant and Chief Master Sergeant. Naturally I was sympathetic with such ambitions, and I felt that Keim was well qualified. I promised to talk to our Squadron Commander, Lt/Col. Ransbottom at Nha Trang, about it. Keim's problem was that our manning document did not provide for the 9 level.

It was a standing joke among the married men, who all agreed with it, to say,
"Now the <u>second</u> thing I'm going to do when I get home is---"
That always got a chuckle, because everyone had about the same idea of what had priority, and that was not to admire the scenery.
Bill Richards, before he left for home, had written to tell his wife that he was learning to play the guitar. She turned the tables on our joke when she wrote back,
"Now, Honey, when you get home, first things first. First of all, I want to hear you play the guitar."
That really got a laugh.

Tuesday, January 17, started off at about 61 degrees. That temperature, combined with cold water, did not encourage a lengthy shower. The wind died down somewhat, but the rain continued. I was glad I'd brought my flight jacket, I wore it all day long.

The weather was no better on Wednesday. Our troops had three different operations going, but we couldn't get up to cover them. However, they had adequate artillery to support them.

The OER that I wrote on Jack Henry "bounced", I got it back that morning. I had rewritten it and planned to fly down to Nha Trang with it in the evening, but the weather forecast en route was so bad that I " chickened out". I had to get it there for sure the next morning, because Scroggin, who had to endorse it, would be there on Thursday for only a few hours, on his way back to the States.

I had been reading the Far East edition of Newsweek with some regularity. I hoped that their reports on US events were more accurate than their reporting of events in Viet Nam. The media were not friends of our servicemen and those patriotic folks we were supporting.

I took off at 0820 Thursday morning, with the redone OER, to get it to the 21st TASS for Scroggin's endorsement when he arrived. For the first few miles, almost as far as Tuy Hoa, the weather wasn't too bad, though I did have a strong tail wind, but the clouds gradually lowered. Finally, for about a ten mile stretch, I had to fly out over the ocean because the clouds were right on the ground over the headland South of Tuy Hoa. I got down to about 300 feet above the water, and it didn't look inviting at all. Then I encountered violent turbulence from the airflow rolling down off the hilltops along the shore. The little O-1 was being rolled clear over on its sides, almost ninety degree banks. I spent about ten minutes exercising every bit of pilot skill I had, very scared. I hoped never to do that again. If the engine had chosen to quit, my only choices were either very rough seas, or the rocky cliff along the shore. In either case my wife would have become

137

a widow right then.

As I approached the farther shore, the turbulence eased off, and I was finally almost able to breathe again. I reached Nha Trang shortly afterward, having set a new O-1 record time en route from Qui Nhon, 1:05.

I got the OER typed up and signed, and ready for Scroggin's endorsement, then ran down some personnel problems for my men, and had lunch. Scroggin was supposed to arrive at 1100, but hadn't shown up yet at 1300. So I went to the Dental Clinic to have the Army Dentist replace a filling that had fallen out the day before. It took about 10 minutes for the novocain to take effect, and 25 more to complete the repair. The Dentist cautioned me not to fly any more that day, because of the novocain. And the weather didn't look good, anyway, so I resigned myself to staying over night, went by the Dispensary to pick up some ointment and the BX to buy a box of stationery.

When I got back to Operations, everyone was standing around looking very glum. I found out why very shortly. Scroggin and another FAC from Pleiku, Maj. Miller, were reported to have gone down, out of gas and lost in the weather, after 4:30 airborne in an O-1, on the way from Pleiku. There wasn't much we could do, since there were already plenty of aircraft out looking for them, so after an hour or so several of us went to the Club (across the street) for coffee.

While we were there, we got word that the missing aviators, probably on their last fumes of gas, had landed at a Special Forces Camp (Green Berets), refueled, and returned to Pleiku. (A tale I heard later said they got lost soon after original take off, and landed over in Laos, at a very hush-hush location, got their tanks filled, and were launched back toward Pleiku to get them out of the area as quickly as possible.)

So I stayed the night in a canvas tent covered hut, with hot water for shave and shower the next morning just next door.

I firmly resolved to never repeat my stunt of the previous morning.

My return to Qui Nhon the next day was uneventful.

Sunday it rained hard again, and I began to worry about

the people in the hamlets out in the valley. I hoped that those in the low areas had gone to higher ground, or had their boats ready. The folks in the hamlets had no radios, telephones or electricity, so they had to do their own weather and flood forecasting. I, at least, was not out risking getting shot or crash landing somewhere.

Monday, nothing new, the rain kept on falling.

Tuesday, Day 199, was a huge success in our housing. We moved some people around, and I finally had the bedroom and office combination all to myself, except for the bed above mine for special over night guests--perhaps Col. Gibson, my new boss at Pleiku. He had replaced Col. Scroggin, who was finally on his way home.

And I could now complete that total one-wall-covering map of Binh Dinh Province and some of the surrounding areas we flew over.

Several of the FAC's went to the Special Forces B Camp (Green Berets) down the street, that night, and got initiated into a Montagnard Tribe, complete with brass bracelets. The initiation rites included sharing straws for a strong drink (Kickapoo Joy Juice?), and taking their shoes off to have their feet sprinkled with some of the same beverage. They missed the really gory parts, which included killing, butchering and barbecuing a cow. They were supposed to go to the Special Forces A Camp at Mai Linh, one day during Tet, for that part.

About January 17, a French woman news reporter, Michelle Ray, had managed to drive up Highway 1 to our 22nd ARVN outpost at English Air Field. There she got her Citroen filled with gas, and announced her intention to drive on up to Hanoi. They tried to discourage her, pointing out that the bridges were out over the river marking the boundary to the next Province. She went on anyway.

She didn't get far. A patrol found her car about ten miles from English a day or so later, concealed off the road, and no sign of her. Her car was towed back to English. On January 25, a captured VC revealed that she had been captured and taken on

Figure 13.1
Northern Border of Binh Dinh Province, Michelle Ray's Citroen Couldn't Pass Here

Figure 13.2
Herb 0-1 at Number 1 (!) Desk

My Year in Viet Nam

up North in the An Lao Valley.

It was amazing, the things that had been coming out of our faucets in the bathroom. Sometimes there was no water, and there hadn't been any hot water for at least three months. But now we were getting numerous baby leeches, parts of bugs, various kinds of dirt, and little red worms. In line with the Army's way of giving out the least desirable jobs, our facilities officer was a second lieutenant. I asked him what could be done to clean up our water supply. He said the water storage tank had to be emptied, undergo a thorough cleaning, and be sanitized. I asked him, why don't we do it? He said he couldn't find the tank, the French hadn't left any information on where it was located.

On Friday, January 27 (Day 202, 163 to go), the day was beautiful all over Binh Dinh Province. I rode in the back seat with Capt. Larry Pritchett, my newest FAC. He was a former B-47 pilot, who had just come from a 4 year tour at the Air Force Academy. He became Herb 10, and in calling the troops he supported on the ground, would say,

" This is Herby Number 10."

The Vietnamese thought that was hilarious, that anyone would call himself Number Ten (the absolute worst).

We noted the news that President Johnson had asked for a 4% raise for Armed Forces Personnel. That we would appreciate, but would the Nation just go deeper in the hole? At the same time, Social Security and income taxes were supposed to increase 6%. I thought we should be concentrating on balancing the National Budget and paying off some of the National debt.

Every one of us who flew a mission on Saturday encountered gunfire from the ground, but we didn't get any holes in pilots or airplanes. The rule of staying at least 1500 feet above the surface was protecting us from small arms fire. Praise the Lord!

On Monday I took our Intelligence Clerk, Airman Liley, who just turned 21 that day, with me, on a trip to a conference in

Pleiku, also taking an airplane to get a fifty-hour inspection. The conference was very productive. I had a theory that our operations were improving by profiting from our predecessors' experiences and mistakes. At least once a year we got a complete change of people. That way the operations didn't stay in ruts for very long. An observant, reasonably talented new man could see the shortcomings of the system much better than could the man he replaced, and he had no face to lose by making changes. So he was much more likely to make them. Col. Gibson was pretty sharp, and had had an excellent chance to appraise the way Col. Scroggin was doing the job. I was very pleased at the way he was tackling the task. My forecast was for much improvement.

On our return flight, we saw vehicle traffic stopped in both directions on Route 19, with about two kilometers between the lead vehicles, a couple of miles East of An Khe. Neither column seemed willing to venture into the space separating them. I circled, but couldn't see the cause of the hesitancy. So I called some ground control agencies to see if they knew or could find out why that piece of the road was thought to be unsafe. No luck. Finally, after I had been circling for 20 minutes, they began moving, advancing through the area from opposite directions at the same time. Who knew? Maybe the sight of an O-1 circling overhead gave them confidence to proceed.

It was pretty dark by then, so after making sure no one was having trouble, I headed on home--another landing with flare pots for runway lights. The Intelligence Clerk was impressed; nothing like impressing a young airman.

My flying time for January was only 48:45, the lowest I'd had for any month since arrival at Qui Nhon. The deficit was all due to the bad weather we'd had. That was still nearly double my average in ten years in SAC, and about four times what I'd been getting at Wright-Patterson. So this really *was* a flying job.

Gib (Col. Gibson) had told the three ALO's he supervised, including me, that we should take time off for leave or R & R at about the four and eight month points in our tours, and that we might not be doing our jobs well if we flew more than 65 hours per month. Well, I had begun planning to take R & R, probably

My Year in Viet Nam

in Hong Kong, at about the 8 or 10 month point; I was already well past the 4 month point. As for flying time, I expected to fly whatever was necessary to get the job done.

He also said he expected to write Outstanding OER's on the three of us, and wanted us to do the same whenever possible for our FAC's.

I finally had enough help to give each of us one day a week off, I chose Sunday. With administrative duties at Pleiku, Tuy Hoa and Cheo Reo, as well as at Ba Gi, I was able to set up a schedule for them, too--Pleiku on Monday, Tuy Hoa on Wednesday, Cheo Reo on Friday and Ba Gi on Saturday. Those worked out well when the flying weather permitted, and no priority at one of them intervened.

My newest FAC was 1/Lt. Dick Hart. On Friday, January 4, I took him to Tuy Hoa, to work with Major Wratten. Dick was Paul Parton's replacement. I continued to Cheo Reo, and had a long visit with Major Clarence Rustvold and Captain Darryl Dixon. Rustvold was scheduled to go on R & R to Hong Kong the following week. He said his wife had given him a long shopping list.

My job had its oddities. I supervised people at a location 45 or 50 miles down the coast, and others 70 or 80 air miles across the jungle. My only communication with them most of the time was by radio. That was no way to get problems discussed, hence my weekly visits. Traveling to either of the other places by road was completely out of the realm of possibilities, so my little executive O-1 Bird Dog was the near perfect solution.

Friends had given me a small battery powered radio, as a way to stay in touch with civilization, before I left Fairborn. Sometimes I couldn't get anything on it, other times it amazed me. One evening I heard a song in German, then one in Dutch. The lady announcer was speaking in some Oriental language.

One morning when I was doing paper work, I had the radio playing nice music when Mama-san came in to sweep or something. She listened for a few moments, then said,

" Oo-oo-ooo! Hanoi!", in a disapproving tone of voice.

The Sunday Collection on February 5 was for Caritas, through which the Bishop of Qui Nhon received help for the poor and the refugees, whom " God must have loved, because he made so many of them".

Monday was routine, but Tuesday was a bit different. I took off early to explore the far Northwest part of the Province for signs of VC activity. I did see some small areas that looked like they could be growing rice. It could have been a few independent folks who did not want to be dragged into the main stream. I was also looking for any signs of a rumored " Ho Chi Minh Trail", with no success. After some hours of looking, I started back to Qui Nhon, then got a radio call from base reporting enemy troops sighted in the area between the Bong Son and English Air Field. At the moment we had no friendly forces in the area. I checked my fuel supply, decided I could detour by there, so I went to take a look. Sure enough I saw individuals and small groups scattered over the area among the houses, hamlets and rice paddies, dressed in NVA uniforms. There was no large enough group to justify calling in an air strike, so I decided against that, and we had no artillery units near enough to reach it. My presence was duly noted by them, however. I saw individuals and small groups scurrying to take cover in the farmers' houses.

I called home plate and reported what I'd seen, and asked that a FAC be sent for some more VR; I was getting pretty low on fuel, and returning.

By the time I got back to Qui Nhon, my bladder capacity was being severely tested, and when I taxied in I was proceeding as rapidly as feasible to one of the white phosphorus rocket shipping tubes we had driven into the sand for relief facilities. As I approached, a man in Army uniform and a female also in uniform jumped in a Jeep and made a hurried departure. The guy must have seen the gleam in my eye.

By the time I got parked, I had logged 5:05, the longest I ever flew an O-1, but still had about 30 minutes fuel left. I had been emphasizing economical operation, but did not want any of my FAC's trying to stay up five hours. About four hours was the most I considered feasible for any of them. I could do it only because I flew mostly at maximum endurance air speed. One of my shorter term FAC's, who had served part of his tour in Laos, said he always flew at 5,000 feet and 100 miles an hour.

There was talk of moving our FAC operation to the new Phu Cat Air Force Base that was being built about ten miles beyond Ba Gi. It didn't look possible before May or so. The Air Field in Qui Nhon was strained to capacity, with us, the Headhunters, the Vietnamese O-1's, lots of Army Huey's and lots of transient traffic. The advantages to us would be better support facilities, and better communications.

Our target markers, Willy Petes, sometimes gave us a surprise. I launched one, one day, and it took off on a long spiral course. The fins were held folded until they emerged from the launching tube, then deployed to provide stabilized guidance. In this case, one fin did not deploy, hence the erratic track.

For a time, supply was not able to send us the white phosphorus rockets, and sent ones deploying various colored smokes instead. They were unsatisfactory because the smoke was much less visible against a vegetation background, and the smoke did not persist.

I was returning from Cheo Reo one day, and heard Joe Wratten from Tuy Hoa call in a strike request for a friendly unit under attack, along a stream some distance North of Tuy Hoa. I flew over to watch, and even got some pictures. A friendly patrol on one side of the stream had come under fire from the other side and asked for help. The fighters arrived shortly, Joe marked the enemy positions, and the fighters did their thing. All the enemy activity stopped, another mission accomplished.

Figure 13.3
    Willy Pete Marker in the Target Area

Figure 13.4
    Bomb on Target

CHAPTER XIV

THE CHINESE NEW YEAR--TET

Tet had arrived. There was supposed to be a truce for the period of celebration of the Chinese New Year, Tet. There were reports of some shooting going on earlier that evening, but I hoped that most of the loud reports I heard were firecrackers.

Later on, every Vietnamese military man in town who had a rifle of some kind evidently wanted to get in the show. There was a lot of gunfire, it sounded like a big war going on, with tracers going across the sky in every direction. I hoped they were all pointed out over the open water, I didn't need any rounds coming through my front wall.

The 22nd Advisory Team gave a little party for the ARVN Officers of the Division. Everyone went around saying,

" Happy Tet!",

which I guessed was a pretty good wish. We talked, had liquid refreshments, and a light snack.

I discovered that in four months Thieu-uy (2/Lt.) Kanh, with whom I worked at Division, would complete four years of military service and become a civilian.

In contrast with him, I talked also to Dai-uy (Capt.) Thuan, the Division Civil Affairs Officer, who had been in continuous military service since 1945. At first he was in the Viet Minh, fighting against the French. But he and many others were disillusioned when they discovered that the Viet Minh was being run by the Communists. So they had come to South Viet Nam either ahead of or with American Dr. Tom Dooley, who had treated many of the refugees from Hanoi when they came South. A large number of the Officers in the South Vietnamese Army, and probably in the South Vietnamese Air Force as well, had come originally from North Viet Nam. Thuan took the long range view; he said that eventually the Communists would destroy themselves. He pointed to the internal mess in China, and to the ongoing struggle between the USSR and China.

Michelle Ray, the French reporter who had been captured by the VC some time back, came walking into the ARVN Battalion dispensary at English, our Northernmost base in Binh Dinh Province, a few miles from where she had disappeared. It was reported that the VC had not physically harmed her, that they had given her receipts for everything they took from her when she was captured, then gave everything back in exchange for the receipts when they released her. They even gave her a ride on a Honda motorcycle to the outpost, over a road they often closed by land mines or by digging trenches across it.

Although she wasn't physically hurt, she was reported to have lost quite a bit of weight, to be pretty badly shaken up, and be very glad to get out of the mess. I gathered she had been in an area or areas where we had put in some air strikes. That probably would scare anyone. I wished it would scare the VC so badly that they would all get rid of their guns and go home.

Tet was the highlight of the year as far as civil celebrations were concerned. Instead of their drab blouses and trousers they usually wore, all the ladies blossomed forth in beautiful, colorful ao dais. The children wore pretty clothes, too. Members of the same family were easily identified by having outfits in the same color and pattern. Apparently the Mama would buy a whole bolt of cloth, and, using her treadle-powered Sinco Sewing Machine, make new clothes for everybody in the family.

Our Intelligence Clerk, Airman Liley, who had flown with me to Pleiku on his 21st Birthday, rode along in our radio Jeep in a convoy to Pleiku, with the radio mechanic from Pleiku, on Thursday morning, leaving at five A. M. They were scheduled to arrive there six hours later, at 11:00. The radios in the Jeep needed some repairs. It would be a great adventure for Liley, I told him to take his M-16 along.

That Thursday morning I was invited to Col. Vong's house for a reception at 0900. Dress was formal, so I broke out my same old summer suit, to wear with tie. Apparently I would represent the US Air Force, I was the only Air Force Officer who been invited that I knew about.

The Province Chief's reception was quite nice. All the US callers wore business suits with ties, as did the Vietnamese callers. Col. Vong was dressed in a light green-blue brocade Chinese man's long gown or coat with black trousers, patent leather fancy shoes, and black open topped turban-like cap. Madame Vong wore a similar long gown of a predominantly dark gray color.

I learned that the house was provided by the government. It was spacious but not plush. It had an open stairway leading to the second floor from the front hallway. There were New Year's greeting cards hanging from the railing, all the way to the top.

We were served small shot-sized glasses of Creme de Cacao in the large formal living room as we walked in, after greeting Host and Hostess. We were also served light wine, dark wine, hot spiced green tea, and little sweet treats--one I identified was candied dried plums.

The whole time I was there, a flock of little kids was peeking in the back door, throwing dud firecrackers to scare us, smiling and laughing. They were so cute I could have grabbed a whole armload of them and hugged them. I didn't think Mother and Daddy, in the formal living room, knew about any of that carrying on behind their backs.

After about half an hour of conversation, with the Vongs and each other, we left, not forgetting to wish the Host and Hostess a most Happy, Healthy and Prosperous New Year.

On Saturday, 11 February (Day 217), Jack Moore was back to see us. He had been appointed the Squadron's wandering inspector, and had to write up all our discrepancies. He was a bit embarrassed at having to come and see us.

Saturday was also the last day of Tet, the last day of truces, back to war on Sunday? After several sunny days, it was raining again that evening.

Tet had been a real holiday. There hadn't even been any farmers in the fields, just a few boys and girls herding their cows. Everyone was all dressed up in Sunday best. And even the little tykes were wearing bright, colorful new pajamas.

To sort of put a spice on things, Nancy Sinatra came to entertain that evening. The performance was in the hangar where Cardinal Spellman had said his Christmas Mass. Considering the risk that I wouldn't even be able to see her, and the likelihood that I'd have a sore back from standing too long, I decided not to go. My reporters said I didn't miss much.

A Korean USO type troupe, three men and three girls, had entertained earlier in the week. They played drums, an electric guitar and a saxophone. The girls made several changes of clothes, and did simple dances. They all sang, the MC had pretty good show-biz English, and the audience enjoyed it.

We honored and wished "Bon Voyage" to an Army Captain who had finished his tour, and was on his way to work on a Master's Degree in Civil Engineering at Stanford. I wondered if he knew what he was in for.

On Monday, I took the leap and ordered a 1967 VW Fastback to be delivered to San Francisco for my pick up any time after July 1, 1967. Optimist?

I was being pressured to select an R & R location and dates, and tentatively settled on Hong Kong. So I wrote to Alberta and asked for a shopping list.

My room took on some additional improvements as an office. I finally got the right wall complete map of the Province up, and even a bulletin board. Of course I still had quite a few visitors in the evenings, both social and business, but most departed by 2200.

I was saddened again by bad news about an airman. I received a call from the Red Cross. They had a letter from a Red Cross Chapter in Texas, saying the Mother of an Airman assigned to us wanted an immediate check on his health and welfare. She had written earlier to tell her son his wife had been " carrying on". The bride of less than a year had had another man living in her apartment with her, and had written the Airman asking for a divorce. Now the mother was worried about the airman working on airplanes, thinking he might be so upset he'd make a mistake endangering someone's life. The young wife had left without leaving any forwarding address.

    I took the Airman to see the Red Cross man who had called, and he talked to him, then showed him his Mother's letter, and asked me to read it. The Airman said he'd like to go home and see if he could straighten things out. I agreed it might be a good idea. I'd be uneasy flying airplanes he worked on if he were preoccupied with personal problems. I recommended that he be given Compassionate Leave, to at least go home and try to cheer up his Mother. Within the hour he was on his way to Nha Trang with my note to the Squadron Commander. I didn't know if desertion by one's wife were sufficient reason for Compassionate Leave. I was sorry for the Airman and his Mother, and his wife. I had a strong desire to kick the guy who moved in with the wife right where he'd never again get such ideas. Odds were that if she got a divorce to marry him he'd lose interest, and be off looking for another pushover to provide free board, room and bed partner. The world might not have been full of such bums, but it surely was over supplied with them.

    Thursday the 16th was a full, busy day. I was up before six, flew 3:40 in the morning, worked various problems on the flight line. The new Senior Advisor, Col. Greer, who replaced Col. Hunter, was not present, but his boss, B/G Lee, from Pleiku, was visiting. I was invited to join him and others for dinner, to help swell the crowd. We had a drink before dinner, then ate with nice china and white table cloth for the occasion, although the food was the same we'd have had in the regular Mess. The power went off, so we finished, romantically (?), by candle light, provided by the Vietnamese waitresses.

    I enjoyed the dinner because Gen. Lee was a very interesting talker, and he did most of the talking. He was the US Army Advisor to Lt. Gen. Vinh Loch, the Vietnamese Army

Commander of II Corps. Lee said Vinh Loch was the most capable General he had met in his career, which had included working for quite a few US generals.

Lee gave us a much broader look at what we were doing than we could have from our own little cubby holes. His analysis confirmed my own cautious optimism, but didn't make the job sound any quicker or easier than I had been thinking.

Lee said we--the Vietnamese, the Koreans, the Americans, the Australians, the Filipinos and others--had been making good progress against the VC. In the time I had been there, the areas of big fights had been moved from less than 30 miles from Qui Nhon to more than 60 in most directions. There were still guerillas around, but they hardly dared be seen in daylight. Their major efforts were directed toward destruction and terrorism. They had assassinated several hamlet chiefs in the last couple of months.

Only that morning they had managed to set off a land mine and blow up a Jeep on National Route 1 about 40 miles to the North. I came upon the scene a few minutes after it happened. The Jeep was upside down over the hole blown in the road, and was completely demolished. I was sure all the people in the Jeep had been killed, but learned later on in the day that no one was even hurt.

The VC must have placed the mine there during the night. Probably the only thing that could eliminate such tricks would be a constant armed patrol up and down the road every few minutes. At night that would be inviting ambush. I wouldn't have wanted the job.

From a problem of not enough pilots, we had gone to a problem of not enough airplanes. We flew those we had so much that they had to be taken to Pleiku or Nha Trang, for inspection, about every week. The inspection at Nha Trang could take three days. We got one airplane back on Wednesday that had to be taken back on Thursday for a new engine. The situation boiled down to only one airplane available at Qui Nhon some of the time. (We needed another Jeep, too). Oh, well, if we'd had everything we needed, we'd have been spoiled.

The airman who " married" the Vietnamese girl, even though he had a wife and four children in Florida, who went on Emergency Leave when his stepfather died, had disappeared. On that same busy Thursday, his Vietnamese "wife", with baby in arms (not his, of course), came looking for him. She said she had given him money, bought him clothes, bought him cigarettes, spent many piastres on him. She wanted to know where he was, and broke down crying. What could we tell her?

We didn't know what her moral standards were, but it was apparently acceptable for non-Christian Vietnamese to have more than one wife. So in her eyes she probably had done no wrong. But along came this character, got what he wanted, and broke her heart.

To try to restrict his unacceptable, irresponsible conduct, the Squadron, at Nha Trang, had called him back there, to be assigned to An Khe, where he wouldn't be able to leave the base. He left Qui Nhon, owing money, but hadn't shown up at either Nha Trang or An Khe. If he didn't get his throat cut out in the countryside, he could have ended up doing time in Leavenworth.

When our power went off, causing the romantic setting for the later part of our Thursday night dinner, it caused the usual situation in our radio room. What General Meyer didn't know, and not likely his successor, Col. McBride, either, was that when we lost power in our radio room, we switched to his independent power supply, via a line from his building to our radio room. When our power went off in the evening, I would some times go to the Radio Room to write letters, courtesy of the Port Commander's generator.

Saturday was a busy day, again. I went to Ba Gi in the morning, and to Pleiku and back in the afternoon. The purpose of that trip was to take some radios for repair, discuss some business with Col. Gibson, and get an airplane inspection. On the way back, I got a call that some friendly troops were being fired upon, so I went by to take a look. When I arrived, the firing stopped, and I couldn't see any unfriendly forces or any source of gunfire, though there were plenty of hiding places, primarily in an abandoned hamlet, all grown up to weeds.

Only the day before I had been called in over some Vietnamese who were being shot at. When I looked at where the bullets were coming from, I discovered more friendly troops, Koreans! They had seen the Vietnamese soldiers, assumed they were VC, and started shooting. Well, I got that stopped. That had happened several times before, when a FAC overhead got friendly troops stopped from shooting at each other. Perhaps we were earning our pay.

I was very impressed with the work ethic in Viet Nam. Most people seemed very industrious. We had a program to put sand bags and sand filled barrels around the aircraft parking places to protect them in case of a mortar attack on the air field. The Army had hired about 30 or 40 young men and women to shovel the sand, fill the sand bags, carry them to position and so on. One day I saw a girl who looked like she was 18 or 19 shoveling sand at a rate few big men could equal. All of them worked almost as enthusiastically. Then I heard that the GI in charge had offered a prize of 200 P for the one who filled the most sand bags. Maybe that had something to do with their enthusiasm.

The cool damp weather had returned to Qui Nhon, but Pleiku that Saturday was hot and dry. Difference? Eighty miles and 2400 feet elevation, even with the same wind direction, northeast. The moist air from the South China Sea left us with all the moisture and dried out in its climb to the Plateau.

Sunday was my day off, and I really made a lazy day of it. But on Monday I went to Nha Trang. It was Air Liaison Officer business, trying to make air support of the Allied Forces work more smoothly and effectively. We (the Vietnamese Forces and their Advisors) had to work out some support problems. I wanted the Vietnamese to know that I, and the Air Support folks, were " on their side". They had many things to learn. The biggest problems the Vietnamese had were not enough trained leaders, professional people, and mechanics. The tremendous resource that the US had in trained people was marvelous from the Vietnamese viewpoint. All the building and aid were helping, but the eventual solution was to get the schools going again, and to provide secondary and higher level education.

The Assignment Clerk at Nha Trang told me I could expect some word on my next assignment some time soon after the first of April.

Alberta sent me a clipping, by a newsman I had met in Ohio, Jim Fain. He wrote about a planned trip to come to Viet Nam to find out about the Pacification Program. Binh Dinh Province would surely be the place to come, because the biggest and most ambitious effort in the country was right there. If he came to Qui Nhon, I could direct him to the Advisors he should talk to. I gave the clipping to US Army Major Galloway, who worked with the Pacification Program.

On Friday morning, 25 February, I was flying when I heard a radio conversation going on about an engagement at Bao Loc, South of us, not in our area, but in the 23rd ARVN Division Area. The FAC was trying to help friendly troops by chasing the VC, firing his M-16, when a rifle round wounded him. He made a forced landing, and a helicopter picked him up, but he died before he could be given medical help. His name was Capt. Wilbanks. I felt very sorry for him and for his loved ones. He had been scheduled to return to the States on March 30.

The 24th Special Zone, based at Kontum, had lost a FAC to ground fire early in my tour.

I had told my FAC's not to try attacking ground forces, the odds would be against them. I surely did not want to lose any of my men.

(NOTE: Capt. Wilbanks was awarded the Congressional Medal of Honor, posthumously.)

On Saturday morning, February 26, my newest FAC, Major Roy Hilliard, went along with me to Pleiku. I had him fly on the way back. He found his way and flew the airplane OK. He had spent the first six months of his tour in 7th Air Force Headquarters at Saigon. He hadn't flown at all for nine months, and said he was glad just to get back in an airplane. His date to return from overseas was the same as mine.

A new scam came to my attention. One of my men was married just before he came to Viet Nam; his girl friend had talked him into it. Of course he made out an allotment in her name before coming. Then the military pay channels found out that she was getting allotments from other " husbands" as well. He discovered he wasn't married after all, polygamy wasn't legal.

Two of the Vietnamese Marines' Advisors came to see us on Sunday evening, and we went to the Club for a beer. When they went out looking for VC, we flew overhead to provide FAC support. They expressed their gratitude for our assistance, and we appreciated their gratitude.

By bedtime, it was wet and cool again, the monsoon had returned.

Everyone using FM radios for communications was assigned a frequency. Because of the importance of keeping our communications open, any interference on our frequency was cause for concern. Nevertheless, our assigned frequency was blocked for a considerable length of time one day by a US Army unit, giving a long " laundry" list of things needed from their supply source--clothing, food supplies, and so on. They apparently could not hear my objections, because they continued for a considerable length of time.

Another time I heard music, as if broadcast by a commercial station, on our frequency. I decided to use the directional feature of the FM, to see where it was coming from. The station was evidently somewhere North of us. Whether it was a deliberate jamming effort, or simply an outlaw use of the frequency, I could not tell.

CHAPTER XV

DOWNHILL FROM NOW ON?

March 1! Day 235--130 to go! I flew 5:15 that day, bringing my O-1 total time to 586:10. In another month I'd exceed my total in B-17's. Gib had told me I should not get more than 65:00 in a month, or I'd be slighting my other work. I got 65:10 in February, so I was delinquent by :10. Thirteen days like March first would put me out of flying time for the rest of the month. So I told my scheduling officer, Phil Jones, not to schedule me for Thursday, the second. He didn't.

In my flying on March 1, I had paid another interesting visit to a Green Beret (Special Forces) Camp. The Special Forces were Montagnard soldiers commanded by US Army Officers and Sergeants. The Montagnards were regarded as very good fighters. The Captain who showed me around said there were at least 500 men trying to get into the outfit, so it must have been considered good duty. He gave me a couple of rations of the kind used by both the US and Montagnard men when they were "in the field". They were completely dehydrated, pre-cooked. Each package contained rice, meat, vegetables, pineapple or orange, salt, pepper, red pepper, tea, consomme' (soup), a vitamin pill, and some very hard candy. The meat varied, of the two he gave me, one had mutton, the other shrimp. Each unit was packed in waterproof plastic and foil, and weighed less than a pound. Two units provided the food requirements for a day, for one man.

This job was teaching me a lot about running an outfit, although there was certainly nothing else like it in the world. Except for the occasional odd ball, such as the one noted earlier, these were all dedicated men with their hearts set on doing their level best. The Air Force had many very fine men, both on the professional level and in the moral sphere. In the wartime atmosphere, drinking or gambling to excess could have been a challenge, but among the more than a dozen and a half FAC's who worked with me, there was never such a problem. What was most gratifying to me personally was their response to my orders and decisions. The men accepted and carried them out without the slightest quibbling or hesitation. That was probably partly due to their knowing I could do any part of the job as well as or better than any of them, that I would not willingly expose any of them to danger unnecessarily, and that I would not ask any of them to do anything that I could not or would not do myself. I didn't have to "order" anyone to do anything. I'd just suggest it or point out the need, and it would get done.

As well as I could judge, morale was high, as was unit pride. The Maintenance Men, the Radio Operators and the Intelligence Clerk were equally as enthusiastic and hard working. We had gripes, but they were about mail, food, facilities and poor equipment, not about each other. I couldn't have asked for a better Command, if that was what it was.

The sun came out for a day or so, but my tentative plan to walk around town to take pictures was headed off by the town's being declared off limits to US personnel, because of possible civil demonstrations. They didn't happen.

The rules by which the maids were paid were changed, we'd now pay them ourselves. The rate was set by the Housing folks. I would now be paying Mama-san the equivalent of about forty-two and a half cents a day. Her pay then varied by the number of men staying in the two rooms. Everything considered, the maids were doing much better than women in other occupations. If we paid more, we'd contribute to inflation. The problem was that there were limited supplies of rice and the other things people wanted to buy. If the price of rice went up, the farmers would be glad, but there was no greater supply of things they wanted to buy, so the price of everything went up. As it was, the market price for rice had about tripled in the past two years. What South Viet Nam needed was not more money, but more production of goods people wanted to buy. The money was no good without something to buy. Basic Economics? It was an interesting study in high school and college, if one just hadn't

My Year in Viet Nam

had to remember names, theories, "Laws", etc.

Chilly, wet weather returned about March 6, and continued for several days, limiting our usual flying activities, some days no flying at all. From the sixth through the twelfth, I logged only 10:35. It was kind of a welcome interlude, in view of the hot weather we knew would return. I used it to advantage to partly catch up on correspondence, both business and personal.

Finally, nearly eight months after my original request, I received a two-drawer safe. And I was even promised a new Jeep!

I decided to pay Mama-san 1500 P. That was a little higher than the standard rate, but my room, doubling as my office, required a little more work. And, when I had an overnight guest, there was an extra bed to make.

Monday, the 13th, I made the rounds to Pleiku and Cheo Reo. I picked up a new FAC, Capt. John Jaczynski, at Cheo Reo. He was scheduled to replace Rustvold when Clarence left for the States on March 27. We'd get him checked out on all the Division procedures, then send him back to Cheo Reo.

The Filipino musical group came again to entertain us that evening. I was reminded of the Filipino band that entertained us at Anderson AFB on Guam, in 1955. Those folks did a really rousing rendition of " When the Saints Go Marching In".

At my request, Gib had brought some brochures for Matson Lines from his R & R in Honolulu. I was working on my plan to take my wife and older son with me on an ocean liner, from Hawaii to San Francisco, on my way home the coming July. They would fly to Honolulu to meet me on July 10. The sailing date for the S. S. Lurline looked the best. I'd have to get my next assignment and my port call date before reaching a decision.

A letter from home brought news and clippings from the Dayton Daily News about a collision between two airliners, with great loss of life, of course. I wondered very seriously if the system I proposed in my Master's Thesis in 1962 would have prevented the collision, as it could have many others. The high powered Government planners were trying to build a gadget that would take over the airplanes and maneuver them to prevent a collision. All a pilot <u>really</u> needs to know is that the other airplane is <u>there</u>. My proposed system would have told each of the pilots another airplane was there, how far away it was, in what direction, and in what direction it was flying. Maneuvering to avoid collision would be an informed decision by the pilot.

Tuesday morning I inquired at Nha Trang about my next assignment. Their information was that I would be working for AFSC as a Staff Development Engineer, base of assignment not yet established. A friend at Andrews AFB said it would be there. Would a letter to the Director of Personnel, Hq. AFSC, requesting assignment to Wright-Patterson, be out of order? Such a request had worked twice before!

I flew in the back seat with Jaczynski, his first ride toward checkout in his new assignment. He would do OK.

We had a meeting of Lt. Cols., starting at 1000 on Thursday, to discuss all the problems of the ARVN system ALO's/FAC's in II Corps. I was the host, and provided coffee and rolls to start off with. The other five were my guests for lunch at noon in the Mess. We had fruitful discussions, and finished our business about 1500. All the others departed with praise for my hospitality, saying also that it had been a good meeting, and my hospitality cost me less than ten bucks.

The weather turned warm, dry and dusty.

I had a sense that I would be leaving the 22nd Advisory Team at the end of my tour with things undone. That would not make me reluctant to leave. I received a letter asking me to consider a six months' extension. NO! Thank you! I was not indispensable.

St. Patrick's Day! Day 251! Only 114 to go!

I spent several hours in a staff meeting and briefing, for an operation planned to begin the next day.

Our ground troops were to begin moving into the An Lao valley the next morning. The An Lao was a tributary coming into the Bong Son from the North, several miles upstream from the highway and rail bridges. The valley had been occupied by the VC for at least three years, with no serious effort made to dislodge them. They could put up a big fight, giving the Air Force FAC's a chance to be big heroes, or the VC might decide to run over the hills into the next Province. If they did that, we would still provide top cover for the operation. Phil Jones and Roy Hilliard were to drive our radio jeep up to the area the next morning, so that we'd have good communications with the FAC's overhead and with our Radio Room in Qui Nhon. They were to park the Jeep right beside the Division's Command Post, so they could work closely with Division. The adjacent air field, English, would also allow quick exchanges of pilots and airplanes.

Some of the airmen had been living in town because they thought the quarters provided by the military were pretty raunchy, though they were probably better than tents. Nevertheless, they'd have to move from town back into the quarters provided, by April first. I expected some griping about it. The objective was to cut down on the amount of money being pumped into the Vietnamese economy, which was causing undesirable inflation.

The initial advance into the An Lao did not stir up much, three men were captured. The other male residents retreated up the valley, so that the only other people taken were women and children. They were moved to a specially prepared camp 75 miles away by road, where they were cared for. They were to be returned to the An Lao Valley when it was considered completely pacified. The male residents were considered to be 100% VC, so they weren't expected to stick around unless they decided to fight. This plan, it was hoped, would influence the men to quit the VC so that they could rejoin their families. This hope was based on the close family ties of the Vietnamese people. That fact had

Figure 15.1 FACs' "Digs" at English Airfield, Protected by Sandbags

Figure 15.2 Montagnard Children at English

My Year in Viet Nam

Figure 15.3
 An Lao Valley, Note Hill and Sand Bar, Upper Center, Phil Jones' Nemesis

been used by the VC in trying to control their neighbors. Now it was being used against them.

I could not help feeling blessed that in America we did not have to suffer the vicious violence and degradation of Communism. (I still pray for the day when the Vietnamese may similarly be blessed.)

On Monday, March 20, events took a turn. Phil Jones was supporting the Vietnamese Marines in their advance up the An Lao Valley that morning. They were taking quite a bit of small and automatic weapons fire from a hillside jutting into the river ahead of them, ending in a sand bar. Their Advisor asked Phil to see, if he could, where the fire was coming from, so they could put some artillery fire on it. Phil found it, all right, he got less than our standard 1500 feet from the hillside, and all the ground fire concentrated on him. He must have taken some rounds in the engine, because it quit. He made a forced landing on the only available spot, the large sand bar on the curve in the river.

I had just started to lunch at 1140 when I got the word that he'd been shot down. I jumped into my Jeep and headed for the flight line, and was airborne by 1200. It was 50 miles from Qui Nhon to the An Lao, and I was there by about 1225. I spotted the O-1 upside down on the sand bar right away. A helicopter, under fire, had just lifted Phil out of the area.

When he had touched down on the sand bar, the wheels did not roll very far before they dug into the sand, and the airplane nosed over, upside down. Luckily, he was between two battalions of friendly Marines. They sent out a rescue party, who got him out of the airplane, and rushed him across the sand to an area sheltered from enemy fire. While they were running across the sand, Phil, with his white flight helmet, over six feet tall, was being laughed at by his rescuers, who probably did not average five feet two or three. When they got to cover, Phil sat down and threw up, and then they really laughed at him. He was lifted out by Army helicopter without either his or any of its crew being hit by the continuing fusillade.

I called the Advisor and asked him if he and his guys

could go back out to the airplane to set it back up on its landing gear, so we could lift it out to English Field by helicopter, for repair. He assured me that they could. I circled while they did it, and THEN he told me they had been continuously shot at the whole time they were out on the sand bar.

After supper that evening, we FAC's, including Phil, and the Marine Advisor who rescued him, had a round of drinks at the Club to toast Phil's good fortune.

The next afternoon I started out on a short flight, in a borrowed airplane, which I had promised not to fly more than an hour and a half. Some of our troops got into a fight, I went to help them, and never did get to where I was going in the first place. Instead I circled over friendly--and enemy--forces for quite a while with only meager success. On the way back to base I heard that a helicopter had picked up our airplane, that was shot down the day before, then accidentally dropped it into the jungle from 2500 feet. Now we couldn't even find it, and probably couldn't repair it if we did. I returned the borrowed airplane after flying it 4:45. So much for promises. We surely did need more airplanes, especially after the loss the day before.

The Far East Edition of Life Magazine for March 6 had an article by Michelle Ray about her visit with the Viet Cong. The area described and the picture of the road were very familiar to me, in the upper An Lao valley. I flew over them several times a week. I might even have been the FAC she saw flying overhead.

Good Friday, March 24, was a long day. I spent from early morning until dark at the forward command post or over the An Lao valley, supporting our troops. The VC were giving way under pressure, not putting up a big fight, but not exactly running, either. I directed a dive bombing strike on some trenches, bunkers, and what looked like tunnel entrances, but I thought the erstwhile residents had moved out. At least we made the fortifications unusable.

I got some depressing news. A FAC with the 24th Special

Zone, Kontum, with a member of the Green Berets in the back seat, crashed right after take off from a Special Forces camp. Both were killed. Kontum had had a FAC shot down and killed only about six weeks earlier. Now there were two more families who would not have a Happy Easter. I was supposed to intercept our Group Commander, Col. Strain, who was a passenger on a C-130 scheduled to land at Qui Nhon some time that evening, to give him the news. After our narrow escape with Phil, I was wishing and hoping more than ever to make it through my year without losing anyone.

Life wasn't all sadness, it still had happy moments. I had always considered the human body one of the most beautiful works of the Creator. Saturday I saw a little girl, about two years old, clothed only in her still perfect innocence, reaching up toward something her Mother was doing. Beauty existed even in the direst circumstances of a war torn land.

Easter Sunday got somewhat complicated. I was scheduled to take off about 1100 to fly to Pleiku for a meeting. But about 1025 I got word that some of our troops were surrounded by VC, asking for our help. So I hurried to the flight line and was airborne about ten minutes early. For nearly two hours I flew over our friendly troops, marking targets for Huey gunships, relaying messages, calling for fighters, and so on. When I got another FAC over the action, I went on to Pleiku.

After the meeting, I returned by way of the scene of the earlier fighting, and found it still going on. I ended up flying nearly an hour after dark. I not only had to keep locating the sources of enemy fire, but had to dodge Army O-1's. I finally exerted my battle area command authority, and told them to fly higher so we wouldn't collide. I had to make sure also, that the Chopper pilots knew where our friendly troops were, so as not to mistakenly shoot at them. I spotted one group of VC especially well dug in, and fired a Willy Pete right into the middle of them, marking them for the Huey gunners.

While all this was going on, some of the Huey pilots were

going in and out under very low clouds to pick up wounded Vietnamese troops. I admired their successful operations in very bad conditions.

I called Roy Hilliard to take my place over the battle area, with Phil Jones set to replace him, then Rex Miller, and then Bob Smith, and so on through the night as long as they needed us. We hoped to enable our ground troops to catch the main force of the VC battalion we thought was in there.

All day long I'd had trouble talking on the radio. I had nearly lost my voice from a cold and sore throat. All the 22nd Advisors knew about my failing voice. Even the Division Medical Advisor had noted my problem, and was going to get me something.

The Viet Cong was in the area to get rice and to try to hinder the Government Rural Development Program, as well as harass or prevent elections scheduled for April. The Panel of Generals governing the Republic of Viet Nam had accepted the new Constitution drafted as the result of the preceding election, and now an election had to be held to select Government officers. The country was making progress. That was bad for the VC cause, so the Communists were going to try to disrupt it. One of the jobs of the Allied Forces was to see that they didn't. That meant that more tough fighting was to be expected.

I got a phone call on Monday saying my next assignment would be at Bolling AFB, Washington. So I prepared and sent another letter reemphasizing my preference for Wright-Patterson. That was my third letter on the same subject. They'd think I was a nut, or stubborn.

Some things took a while to materialize. On Tuesday afternoon, a big executive office chair was delivered to my Office (also bedroom). It was at least as fancy as President Johnson's. It swiveled, and tilted back, with walnut frame, and had leather back, seat and arm rests. The spring in the tilt mechanism allowed it to be pushed back just far enough to let me put my feet up on the desk. Some of the men thought it would be just right for an afternoon nap (or for thinking, if someone were looking). Mama-san, of course, called it Number One. Also on Tuesday I received a package of Contac from the Radio Operators at Tuy Hoa. They had noted my difficulties talking on Sunday.

My R & R to Hong Kong for about the 12th of April was approved. I began looking forward to it.

Supply broke down and brought more chairs, (more places to sit for our evening briefings) and a refrigerator. Now I'd finally be able to start enjoying the Kool Aid Alberta's sister had sent me months before.

I finished March with 70:30 for the month, 5:30 over Gib's established limit. He didn't say anything about it. I now had 651 hours in the O-1, the most I'd ever flown in a like period of time. Indeed this was a <u>flying</u> job.

I also had a short call from my wife (amazing that she got through) saying our friend in the DC area had called to report that my request for assignment back to Wright-Patterson was being honored. I must have snowed 'em under.

Sunday, 2 April 1967, Day 267, 98 to go! A letter came to confirm my next assignment:
" I am pleased to inform you, if you do not already know, that you will be assigned to Wright-Patterson AFB, Ohio, upon your return from overseas in July 1967, in AFSC 2811.
" Sincerely,
    (Signed) Albert Dauth
    Albert Dauth, Lt. Colonel, USAF
    Chief, R & D Officer Manning Division
    Directorate of Military Personnel"

AFSC 2811: Staff Development Engineer, Entry Level

That evening we had a party for M/Sgt Keim, who was being transferred to Nha Trang. We'd had a party for three other maintenance men who were leaving, just before Easter. We didn't know then that Keim was leaving. My pleading for him with the Squadron at Nha Trang must have helped.

We had the party at our Maintenance building on the flight line. It was only about 25 feet from the cyclone fence surrounding that part of the airfield. Just outside the fence were a lot of shacks made of sticks and cardboard boxes that refugees lived in.

That evening one of our men had brought a portable TV, and set it up out in back next to the fence. It attracted a crowd of about 50 or 60 people, mostly kids, on the other side of the fence. It received only Armed Forces Network, whose transmitter antenna was on the hill above the airport. It was probably the first time any of them had ever seen TV. The little tykes were especially enthralled. I took a couple of flash pictures of the audience.

Guests at the party were three US Marines, who acted as Advisors to the Vietnamese Marines to whom we had been providing air support. They were enthusiastic in their praise of our help. We were most appreciative of their praise.

The Sergeants who were leaving obviously thought they were leaving a fine outfit. I had never seen any kind of a unit with higher morale or greater enthusiasm for the job they did. I sneaked in a hope that I might have had something to do with it. My attitude to all the men was that I respected each for what he was, and confidently expected each to do his best in his immediate job and for the team effort. I tried never to be too busy to chat with a man and to explore his interests and his problems. They responded with courtesy, respect and apparently genuine liking.

My trip to Nha Trang the next day was eventful in that I found out at Personnel that the information saying that I was going to RTD at Bolling, had been a misinterpretation of the assignment code, it really said AFSC at Andrews. But they didn't yet have the news I'd gotten from Dauth. The TASS Commander, Lt. Col. Ransbottom, thought I might be able to get my reassignment travel date moved up a few days.

That evening we were invited to the International Control Commission Headquarters in Qui Nhon for a cocktail party

Figure 15.4
Watching TV through the Fence

honoring the departure of the Canadian member, and the arrival of his replacement. There was also a member from India and two from Poland. I chatted for quite a while with the Indian member, but could not seem to pronounce or spell his name.

When John Kaczynski, my new FAC at Cheo Reo, first came, he told me that his wife had been " mugged" in Brooklyn, where she lived, and was pretty upset mentally. On Wednesday, the fifth, a TWX came from her doctor, saying she was seriously ill with mental problems, and asking that John get there as soon as possible. So he left immediately on Emergency Leave.

My past was catching up with me. In Distribution from the 21st TASS was a Citation for the Air Force Commendation Medal, for my work with the B-58 Flight Control System. There wasn't any medal with it. I could carry it back to Wright-Patt and turn it in to Personnel. I didn't know if they would give me a medal to go with the citation or not.

I heard that the US Army Advisors and Headhunters had put Larry Pritchett and me in for some kind of awards for the action on Easter Sunday, and I was scheduled to appear at two different places on Monday morning, April 10, for some kind of Vietnamese awards. Meanwhile, the Army Bird Dog pilots had named me an honorary Head Hunter, and gave me a shoulder patch attesting to same.

The next day, Major Dick Smith arrived as our newest FAC. Major Bob Smith, already one of us, said that with a name like that, Dick was bound to be a good man. My plan developed quickly; I'd get Dick checked out and assign him as the Sector FAC at Cheo Reo. If Jaczynski returned, we'd hold him at Qui Nhon.

My optimism continued--I sent a check to pay for the new VW Fastback that was scheduled to be waiting for me in Frisco.

Life had its funny moments. One morning I was flying overhead a small Vietnamese unit. Their Advisor was kind of jittery because VC had been reported in the area, so I was looking carefully. I saw a man running across a paddy, and reported it to the Advisor. His response?

" Oh! That's one of our guys. He's chasing a chicken he's trying to catch for his lunch."

In that same area were sections containing large numbers of big jars, twenty or thirty gallon capacity, they looked like earthenware. Were they for rice storage? When I flew over the area later, it looked like they had all been deliberately broken by someone.

I got into a conversation one day with a South Korean civilian. He was working for a construction contractor. He said the job paid better than anything he could get at home, and he was able to save most of his pay. His ambition was to start up a private business back in Korea, and hopefully be able to make his fortune. Was that war profiteering?   No, I thought it was simply promoting Capitalism.

CHAPTER XVI

DOWN WHERE THE PEOPLE LIVED

Finally I took my Sunday off to explore Qui Nhon. One of the sites was the Qui Nhon Market. All kinds of things were sold there, but the major items were food, some to be eaten there, some to be taken home. The place was indescribably dirty, overcrowded, primitive, swarming with flies. There were almost no packaged foods, most things were sold in bulk. The fresh fruits and vegetables with skins, such as oranges, bananas, limes and tuberous vegetables, probably could be used safely, as could the dried foods, like beans and rice, that needed cooking. However, there were big open containers of spaghetti, soup and vegetables for sale and consumption on the spot. Fresh meat was spread out in the open, where flies could get on it and anyone could pick it up and examine it. With no refrigeration, the meat of animals butchered in the morning had to be cooked and eaten that day. I knew it had not been inspected, either. Probably least appetizing of all were eggs with part of the shell chipped away to show the baby chick that had been growing inside.

Not to be overlooked were the US Army supply items, like canned goods and Washington Apples that were also on display. They were not legal items of trade, but it was hard to even guess how many devious transactions they had been through before showing up for sale by some pitiably poor merchant.

There were also all kinds of pots, pans, dishes, notions, cosmetics, clothing, brooms, and so on, for sale.

What it brought home to me was a realization of the tremendous value of our organized, regulated food production and distribution system, still under free enterprise. If the Communists could have cleaned up that market, they'd have appeared to be doing the country a lot of good. Of course their way would have been to start off by putting all the little merchants out of business, and making the whole thing a state owned operation. They might have been more sanitary and efficient, but nobody would have been his own boss, and where could one

Figure 16.1
Cathedral Interior

Figure 16.2
Cathedral Side Altar

My Year in Viet Nam

Figure 16.3
　　Children Leaving Cathedral After Children's Mass

Figure 16.4
　　Fabric Shop

have gone to haggle and bargain?

My visit to the Cathedral on a Sunday morning was much more edifying. Like almost any Catholic Church in the world, it was a quiet, restful place, yet warm and alive with the Divine Presence. There was need of paint, and birds freely came and went, but the floor and the simple pews were clean. The people who were putting things in order after the Children's Sunday Mass (even a group of 8 to 10 year old girls) were quiet and reverent, and the sounds from outside, although the doors were open, were muffled. There were a few statues, but no stained glass picture windows, no expensive frescoes or paintings, very few decorations of any kind, but I thought it lovely.

My walk along the main street of the town was enlightening but uninspiring. There were simple open shops, catering to the every day needs of the people. One shop could only be described as a hardware store. It dealt in things of metal, and simple tools. One display featured varicolored plastic covered wire clothes hangers. There were also cooking utensils of various kinds.

There was a fabric shop displaying bolts of cloth of all colors and varied patterns, a meter wide, and sold by the meter in length. Adjacent to it was a shop specializing in foot treadle powered Sinco sewing machines. Those two shops together explained the origin of all the pretty clothing seen at Tet and other holidays.

I had seen sugar cane growing out in the rural area, and had seen bundles of it stacked along the road. Now I discovered where some of it went. A four-wheeled towable vehicle sitting on the street had a service counter built on it, with a canopy, and a hand operated press mounted at one end. There was also a supply of sugar cane stalks. For a refreshing drink, one paid a couple of piastres and received a glass of freshly squeezed sugar cane juice. When finished with the glass, the customer returned it, and it was filled for the next client, without benefit of any kind of washing from one to the next. I didn't have any.

There were also street vendors much like in Saigon. One lady with her chogey stick carried two baskets of fresh fish. They

My Year in Viet Nam

Figure 16.5
    Hardware Store

Figure 16.6
    Sinco Sewing Machine Store

My Year in Viet Nam

Figure 16.7
    Sugar Cane Juice Sales

Figure 16.8
    Fresh Fish for Sale

evidently came from one of the fish traps we saw from the air out in the shallow part of the harbor.

One lady specialized in selling hard candy.

There was one shop at which one could buy his own coffin, marked with his choice of religious symbols, Buddhist, Cao Dai or Christian.

None of the vendors wore fancy clothing, just the black trousers and, loose shirt by the men, or subdued color blouse by the women.

There were quite a few light trucks, lots of bicycles, and there were Lambrettas (three wheeled powered vehicles), various motor scooters, but very few cars. At the main intersection was a sheltered small stand for a traffic policeman directing traffic. There was also an Esso gas station.

There was lots of sand available, and one man, with a sack of cement, was making concrete blocks. At another pile of sand, small boys were having a great time playing in it.

As I walked along the street, I met two young ladies, probably about ten or twelve years old, with a basket of home made (lye(?)) soap, in their conical straw hats and modest blouses and trousers, selling the soap for their mothers. I didn't buy any, but they very graciously posed for their picture.

Farther along I encountered half a dozen boys who joined me, chattering and grabbing my hands. I discovered that one of them was trying to remove my wrist watch. When they saw that I had realized what was going on, they scattered.

An interesting sight was a stack of empty artillery shells several feet high, covering most of a block. No doubt they were being saved as salvageable scrap metal.

The main occupation in the rural areas was the production of rice. The process began by plowing each paddy with oxen or water buffalo power. Often there was water standing in it when it was plowed. Rice seedlings were grown in small plots, then set by hand in the freshly prepared, flooded paddies. This work was often done by girls who would be in High School in the USA. From then until the crop was nearly ready for harvest, the

Figure 16.9
Coffin Shop

Figure 16.10
Qui Nhon Main Intersection

Figure 16.11
Basic Transportation, a Lambretta and a Trike

Figure 16.12
Girls Selling Soap

major work was to keep the individual paddies flooded. In some areas, the water could be diverted from flowing streams, in others it had to be lifted into each paddy by some other means, often by back breaking labor. In some cases it was by bucket between two men, sometimes it was by foot pedaled water wheel. I saw one gasoline engine powered pump. As the crop neared the ripening stage, the water was drained out, allowing the crop to mature.

The crop was cut by individual hand sickles and tied into small bundles with rice straw. In the Qui Nhon area, it was then carried by chogey sticks to the farmer's farmyard, where it could be sheltered from the rain, and allowed to dry. Then it was hand threshed by beating the heads of each bundle on a wood lattice to knock the grain out, and the grain gathered underneath. Then it might be further dried on a clean, dry surface, such as a spot on the road.

In one area I saw, in another Province, small portable inclosed boxlike structure was carried by two men, from one paddy to another. A person stood at one side of it and beat the heads on a lattice inside the box, to thresh the rice, letting it fall to the bottom of the box. That obviated carrying the straw to the farmyard.

Once the crop had been harvested, the procedure could begin all over again. Since there was never any frost, it was possible to grow as many as three crops a year on the same paddy.

Much to my surprise, corn was also grown in some parts of the Province. However, it was not flooded. Its ripening was not even and all at one time, because frost never comes to kill the stalks.

Since there was no such thing as natural gas or electricity, cooking was done over a small grate, burning wood or charcoal. Small bundles of wood sticks were available at the markets.

When the rickety houses were open in the daytime, I could see where the families slept, on flat wooden sleeping platforms with no such thing as mattresses, just thin pads, with thin substitutes for blankets. I also noted the family dogs covered with scabies, which some of the children had, too.

My Year in Viet Nam

Figure 16.13
   Plowing for Rice

Figure 16.14
   Moving to the Next Paddy

My Year in Viet Nam

Figure 16.15
Transplanting Rice, One Seedling at a Time

Figure 16.16
Rice Transplanters

My Year in Viet Nam

Figure 16.17
Lifting Water to a Paddy

Figure 16.18
Rice Bundles Ready to Carry to the House

I finally got around to visiting the Leprosarium just a few miles down the coast. On the way there I met a man carrying two large bundles of dead wood tree limbs down the hill into town, destined, I was sure, for the cooking grates of families in Qui Nhon.

I was greeted at the front door of what appeared to be the main Leprosarium building, by a Vietnamese nun. She said something in broken French, and left. Another nun who came said,

" Un moment, I get Sister."

The next one who appeared greeted me heartily in a Cockney accent direct from London, England. We conversed very successfully. She told me the Leprosarium was operated by a Sisters of Charity Order from France. I mentioned Msgr. Feiten's name, and the nuns recalled him and his Bishop enthusiastically. The English Sister gave me a tour of the whole facility. It sat next to a beautiful beach. Sister told me they had formerly welcomed US service men to come and use the beach whenever they chose, but the guys trashed it with paper waste, empty bottles, etc., so that the beach became a mess. The residents were sick people, and just couldn't keep up with cleaning it, so that finally the Sisters had had to ask the US commanders not to let their men come there to use it any more.

When someone developed leprosy, the whole family would come to the Leprosarium, so that the disease could be treated and kept from spreading to other members. The living quarters were set up for families.

There was a new family unit they proudly showed me, with a sign saying it was a gift of the Feiten Family and Bishop Feiten in America. (In translating, Monsignor meant Bishop in French, so Monsignor reverted to Bishop when it was translated back to English.)

One wing was set up with rooms for single men. And new construction for additional housing for patients was under way, the labor of patients who were able to work.

The main facility was beautifully done in tile, with central

Figure 16.19
Bringing in Wood for the Cooking Fires in Qui Nhon

Figure 16.20
The Feiten House

Figure 16.21
    Sanitizing Cooking Pots

Figure 16.22
    Leprosarium Tile Makers

Figire 16.23
New Command Chapel in Qui Nhon, Tiles Donated by Leprosarium

Figure 16.24
Gift for Monsignor Feiten

gathering areas, One activity going on was a pot cleaning session. Each family was required to bring in its cooking pot each morning for cleaning and sanitizing. In another area, classes for the children were being conducted.

Sister showed me their tile making facility, being operated by men with leprosy. I ventured that this must be a money-making operation. She said they did not sell their tiles, because they could not commit to either numbers or delivery times, so they gave them to their friends. One of their beneficiaries was the new US Armed Forces Chapel in Qui Nhon, beautifully tiled.

Sister told me that the Viet Cong had never bothered them, probably because they did not want to expose themselves to the disease.

The Sisters asked me if I expected to see Msgr. Feiten, and I told them his sister was a very good friend of our family, and we would be sure to visit her family. So they gave me a beautifully wrapped package for Msgr. Feiten. They did not tell me what was in the package.

CHAPTER XVII

R & R TO HONG KONG

On Day 276, only 89 to go, April 11, my long anticipated Rest and Recuperation Leave began. The first leg was by an old C-47 to Cam Ranh Bay. It took me all of thirty minutes to get processed in there and get some ice cream from the ice cream truck. Then I caught a 5-mile bus ride to the VOQ, new raw wood barracks in hundreds of acres of deep sand. It took a few minutes to get registered to get a bed for the night.

At the nearby Club I talked for some time to an Army Major who was just returning from R & R in Malaya. He reported that five days and nights had cost him about $60. He was single, and didn't do a lot of shopping, but had had a marvelous time. He said his most expensive dinner had cost him two dollars.

The next morning I got up too late for breakfast. Then I changed my Mickey Mouse money into genuine American dollars, so I didn't have any acceptable money to buy lunch.

Just after noon I boarded a DC-6, (four propellers), to Hong Kong. "Sixes" had once been the mainstay of the airlines, but they were being replaced by jets. This one was still real luxury, and the in-flight dinner was great--fresh fruit cocktail, broiled steak with parsley and butter, buttered string beans, croquette potatoes, mixed salad with dressing, rolls with butter, dessert, and coffee, tea or milk; I chose the milk, hadn't had any for-- how long?

An optical illusion--the blue South China Sea with no whitecaps, and just a few white clouds below us, looked like the sky, so that we seemed to be flying upside down. Then I noticed the regular blue sky in its regular place, with a few cumulonimbus clouds around the horizon.

We saw a few ships, but they looked quite small from our altitude. I was used to seeing things as much larger, such as children, ducks, and even wires, from O-1 altitude.

We arrived at the Hong Kong Airport about 4:30 p. m. It was interesting because the runway is built on material brought

Figure 17.1
    Cam Ranh Bay Area

Figure 17.2
    Barracks and Latrine, Cam Ranh Bay

from the island areas nearby that had been cut down to make room for the many tall buildings. It was a man made peninsula on which was built the runway surface, water off both sides and off the "far" end.

We had an R & R briefing to tell us about all the many things we could spend our five days doing. Shopping was emphasized, but there were also sights to see and tours to take. We were urged to go to the China Fleet Club shopping center to compare quality and prices before buying much of anything. We exchanged a hundred US dollars for Hong Kong dollars, and they held out enough for our transportation from and to the airport. The exchange rate was HK$5.70 per US$1.00

I chose to stay at the Hong Kong Hilton because it was the best in town, and only about $3.40 a day more a day than the next less expensive one.

After getting settled in, I showered in HOT water (there wasn't any <u>cold</u>), and no little red worms came out of the faucets! Having freshened up, I went for a walk through part of the city near the Hilton. I passed a number of banks, offices of steamship and airlines companies, and offices of big companies from all over the world. Most of the people I saw were Chinese, although there were quite a few Caucasians, particularly in the hotel.

I was able to call my wife on a commercial telephone line, and tell her to put a couple hundred in my Kelly Field National Bank account, as a shopping cushion. The system was a lot better than MARS, we could even hear each other!

I had planned to buy a business suit in Hong Kong, but the tailors had gone on strike, so that was out. After a sort of a warm up on Thursday, I really got into shopping on Friday, watches for the family, beautiful dress material, a 108-piece set of crystal, etc.

Hong Kong and The new Territories were a British Crown Colony, by agreement at the end of the Boxer Rebellion. It was scheduled to revert to China in 1997. As a trade center of the Orient, it was much favored because its highest tax rate was 15%.

Hong Kong sits on an island, across the harbor from Kowloon and the New Territories. There were ferries between

Hong Kong and Kowloon. In two days I rode the ferry six times for a total cost of HK$1.50, about 26 cents US. The London style double decker buses cost 20 cents HK, about 3 1/2 cents US.

    Friday night I took a conducted tour of "Kowloon After Dark", with Lotus Tours.

    Four of us R & R'ers rode in a Mercedes 190D, our driver and tour leader was Jackie, a Chinese young man from Shanghai. He told us the primary language in Hong Kong was Cantonese, and he had lived in Canton as well as in Shanghai, where he had graduated from high school. He had been in the Colony for about ten years.

    He also understood some Mandarin, and was pretty good in English. So he was somewhat of an accomplished linguist, as well as a good driver. He said the Mercedes 190D was a popular car for taxis and for tours. It cost over US$4,000, but got 35 miles per Imperial gallon of diesel fuel (cheaper than gasoline) and was very durable, as well as easy riding.

    Jackie told us 98% of the people in Hong Kong and the New Territories were Chinese, 60% had come from the mainland since the Communist take over. 40% of Hong Kong's people were under 16 years old. The many dialects spoken in China were not mutually understood by the speakers--someone from Shanghai would not be able to converse with someone speaking only Mandarin or Cantonese. However, since writing and printing used pictographs instead of sound symbols, newspapers and books were readable everywhere--just the word sounds were different.

    Jackie's father had once owned and run a shop in Shanghai. Now the government owned the shop, and his Dad just worked there.

    Jackie told us that *free,* public, *mandatory* schooling there was not. He or she who went to school had to pay for it, "public" school or otherwise. Tuition averaged about HK$15 per month, and students had to buy their own books and uniforms. So, the poorer children often did not get to go. Admission to the limited higher education level schools was by passing exams.

    The average factory wage was HK$1.00 per hour, and

My Year in Viet Nam

Figure 17.3
Public Housing, Kowloon

Figure 17.4
House Boats, Hong Kong Harbor

the work week was seven ten hour days. Jackie said Hong Kong had mostly poor people and rich people, with very few middle class. The rich people lived in the high rise apartment buildings, with rents from HK$1,000 per month on up. Many of the "poor" people lived in government owned public housing, at US$2.50 to US$15.00 per month.

Back to the evening tour--it began with dinner in a Chinese restaurant, Chinese style. It was well patronized by Chinese people, all well dressed. When a group ate together, each ordered only one or two dishes, and then all shared them, family style. A person alone ordered only one or two dishes, servings were all about the same size. We had steamed chicken, sweet and sour pork, a similar beef dish, fried rice with egg and shrimp, egg foo young, steamed small shrimp, and Chinese spaghetti with squid. After some initial clumsiness, chopsticks worked o. k. Most of it tasted good to me, washed down with hot tea, and my digestive tract had no trouble at all.

After dinner we went to a hill overlooking the cities, the airport and the harbor, to admire the view, then to an amusement park. It featured roller skating (on concrete), games of chance, bowling, a zoo, rides, and free Chinese opera in different theaters. We learned that each theater had a different program each evening, and each performed in a different Chinese dialect. We saw parts in Cantonese and Mandarin. The acting was stylized and tended to be symbolic.

From the park we went down to the Market, which occupied 2 1/2 miles of Temple Street in Kowloon. One could buy anything imaginable there, and some things I had never imagined. One could have his fortune told by a bird, buy California oranges, radios, clothing, "jewellery" (British spelling), barbecued snake, and " hundred-year-old" eggs, One could play mah jongg in dozens of places, and so on and on. The sounds, sights and smells were--well, exotic?

From Temple Street we went to the Kingsland Night Club, a very posh place in one of the big hotels, with a floor show reminding me of Forbidden City in San Francisco. First drink (all I had) was on Lotus Tours.

My Year in Viet Nam

Figure 17.5
Temple Street, Downtown Kowloon

Figure 17.6
Kowloon Children

The floor show was strictly American, fresh from Las Vegas, probably with more clothes than they wore in Vegas, doing various athletic and acrobatic dances; they had a so-so singer, too.

After the show ended, the tour was over, Jackie took me back to the ferry, and I returned to the hotel and to bed.

In the course of my walking around seeing the sights, I took quite a few slide pictures. Whenever the views included people, they hid their faces or turned their heads. I was told that they thought that if one took their pictures, he also took their souls. " The eyes are windows of the soul." If their eyes were hidden, you couldn't take their souls.

Saturday morning I took a boat tour of the harbor. There were ships of many nationalities, the kind of junks I had seen pictures of, and some British warships. Perhaps more interesting were the small boats propelled by individuals, man, woman or child, working a long oar over the fantail, propelling them in much the same fashion as fishes' tails do. One middle size boat carrying a load of sand was propelled by a slow running, one-cylinder gasoline engine. It sat so low in the water that a small wave would have capsized it.

In one area of the harbor there was a large flotilla of house boats, on which people lived. I guessed they'd have to fish the kids who fell overboard out of the water now and then. The hillsides otherwise unoccupied had large numbers of the same kind of shacks to be seen around the end of the runway at Qui Nhon.

Sunday morning I went to Mass at the Church of Our Lady of the Rosary, in Kowloon. Everything was in Chinese, but the ritual was the same as at any other Catholic Church in the world. The priest was European, but read his sermon in Cantonese. I learned some Cantonese, "Alleluia" came out "ah-lay-loo" , "Amen" became "ah-mah".

Sunday afternoon I took another tour with Lotus, and lucked out, having Jackie as guide again. There was only one

My Year in Viet Nam

Figure 17.7
Hong Kong Water Taxi

Figure 17.8
Water Pipes from China, New Territories

other passenger, a lady Civil Servant from 7th Air Force Headquarters in Saigon.

We drove out into the New Territories beyond Kowloon, and saw such things as a pig being taken to market, nosed into a pointed basket tied closed behind his rump, in a wheelbarrow. A much bigger one got to ride in a four wheeled cart with two pushers.

There were many small truck garden plots, growing Chinese preferred vegetables, the kind we saw in the markets in Hong Kong and Kowloon. Near the border with Red China, we could look over into the other country. A very interesting feature was two parallel pipelines, six or eight feet in diameter, that carried fresh water into the Colony. I concluded Red China must have liked the way the political picture was, they could have exerted their will at any time by threatening to cut off Hong Kong's and Kowloon's water supply.

We stopped for afternoon tea at a sort of local touristy restaurant, where everyone seemed to be enjoying the beautiful Sunday afternoon--far from war.

With sore feet (blisters on blisters) and empty bank account, I left Hong Kong on Monday morning, and arrived at Nha Trang, via Cam Ranh Bay, on Monday evening. I stayed overnight, to once more verify my next assignment, back to Wright-Patterson, and caught a C-123 on to Qui Nhon the next day. What a marvelous little vacation that had been!

Noted in passing: Cam Ranh Bay was not only the location of a busy airport, but was also a busy seaport, which lent great assistance to the war effort.

CHAPTER XVIII

BACK TO WORK AGAIN

" Back in the saddle again" didn't take long. After Wednesday off to catch my breath, I flew two hours in the back seat with a new FAC on Thursday, two more hours after dark on Thursday night, and flew again on Friday.

Friday night we had a beer, chicken and hamburger party at the flight line, and invited some of our Army counterparts. They appeared to have a good time, too. No up front cost--the profits from a little pop and beer selling enterprise at Operations paid for it. The party was at a good time, lights were off in Quarters until after ten o'clock.

I took my two newest FAC's, Captains Bob Buckles and Jimmie Nelson, with me to Division Headquarters at Ba Gi on Saturday morning. They received a special briefing on the military situation in the 22nd Division area. Bob was slated to remain at Qui Nhon, replacing Capt. Miller, who went to Kontum to replace the FAC who was killed there. Jimmie was to go to Cheo Reo. I sort of rejoiced that I didn't have as long to go " in country" as they did.

I had planned to go to Mass at the Cathedral on Sunday morning, but the town was off limits for Americans until Tuesday, for another election, this time to choose representatives to the National Assembly. The US was doing everything possible to avoid getting involved in Vietnamese politics. I went to the Mass upstairs from my quarters, and found myself Lector as usual.

We were scheduled to get another new FAC. How different from last August--we still had the same number of airplanes, but now three times as many FAC's.

Well! Here it was, April 27, Day 292, only 73(?) to go!
It was a hectic day. I got into a big hassle with a Lt. Col. of the First US Air Cavalry. To say the least, he was arrogant. I had plenty of reason to get angry at him, but held my " cool".

I had gone by myself to the Cav. forward command post,

and very quickly got outnumbered. But I got to the root of the problem, so something was accomplished, even if the problem wasn't solved. The L/C said he was going to the Cav's Commanding General. That was supposed to scare me, but Generals didn't scare me, especially US Army ones. I'd made my last promotion anyway. I hoped that on the morrow I could talk the matter over with Col. Hieu and his Deputy, Lt. Col. Ly.

The First Cavalry's problems with us and the 22nd would have been solved if they showed some good sense, and operated the way they were supposed to. They acted like they were in charge of the whole show. They were not. Oh, well, I couldn't stew and fret too long, I was scheduled to fly at 0630 the next morning.

That was a long day, too. I flew over to Cheo Reo, and rode in the back seat with Capt. Jimmie Nelson, while he directed air strikes to complete his check out. I had him fly me back to Ba Gi then, where I spent a large part of the afternoon in conference about the problem that the First Cavalry complained about the day before. We thought we came up, finally, with a way to solve it without making anyone mad.

In the evening there was an election of officers and approval of a Constitution for a new Officers' Club in Qui Nhon, with free beer and fried chicken dinner afterward. Only Army Officers were Active (voting) Members; all other US and foreign officers could join as Associate members. The Army was pretty " snooty" about such things.

Saturday night I learned something new, to me at least. I met the new Chairman of the International Control Commission for the Qui Nhon area, another Officer from the Army of India. He was the same rank as I, (O-5), but the British term was " Half Colonel". I thought I liked the Vietnamese term, " Trung-ta", as well or better.

Being the commander of a local Air Force contingent had its interesting, and sometimes entertaining, moments. One of our Airmen was cited for passing, in a Jeep, when there was an oncoming vehicle, on Saturday morning, and that same evening went to the Airmen's Club on the Flight Line, where he was drinking. After while he had to go to the bathroom, and decided to go back to quarters for that purpose. He "borrowed" an Air Force ton and half truck for the trip. When he returned to the Club, the MP's were waiting for him. Lt. Col. Rutherford, commander of the unit owning the truck, was notified, and the Airman was pretty badly scared when he came in to see me. He was also still somewhat the worse for the alcohol, and was all ready to cry. He was afraid he would be court-martialed or reduced in rank, or both. I told him to go to bed, and I would talk to Col. Rutherford to see what action he planned to take. I knew Rutherford slightly, and thought him pretty reasonable. I thought we could agree to allow the Airman one mistake. I also thought the incident should teach the Airman that drinking could get him in serious trouble.

I finished April with only 51:50 flying time, well within Gib's guidelines. Of course my visit to Hong Kong had something to do with that.

On May 1, I flew 2:45 with our newest FAC, Capt. "Dusty" Coyner. He didn't enlighten us on the reason for the nickname.

I talked with Col. Rutherford, and as I expected he was quite congenial about the whole affair concerning the Airman's borrowing the truck. But I let the Airman think he just barely escaped serious consequences, in the hope he would steer clear of similar behavior in the future. He looked almost as shaken up when I told him he was off the hook as he did the night before when he came to say he was in trouble. He was barely 21, his parents were both living, and he evidently regarded them highly, and with affection. I was old enough to be his Dad. Was I sort of a father figure?

Also on May 1, I got official word confirming my reassignment back to the Aerospace Systems Division at Wright-Patterson. That was reassuring news about my future in the Air Force.

We had another party at the flight line, barbecued steak and chicken, potato salad, pop and beer. I even saw a bottle of bourbon. Airman Liley finagled the steaks from men on the cargo ships in the harbor.

Our parties on the Flight Line fairly often had a kind of special guest, an Air Force Flight Nurse who flew with a C-141 Medical Evacuation aircraft. She seemed to enjoy our company more than that of the Army Nurses at the local Army Hospital. She'd come to see us whenever her crew came to pick up patients to return to the States. She was not very big, and was fun to visit with. We kind of adopted her, and called her " Charlie Brown", in honor of the Peanuts Comic Strip.

After I got back to quarters following the party, I was writing letters when the lights went out. I ended up writing by flashlight reflected off the ceiling.

The weather was getting a little warmer every day, the heat of July would soon return. And, I'd be going home to escape most of it!

May 2 and 3 went somewhere, and here it was, Ascension Thursday, May 4, 299 days gone, and only (about) 66 to go. Because of the religious holiday, Mama-san took the day off, and I made my own bed. One of her Buddhist buddies did the house keeping for the day, and Mama-san would return the favor on Buddha's birthday, May 23 or 24.

It was another busy day; I flew a mission on the way to Pleiku for an airplane inspection, back to Qui Nhon, then to Nha Trang for inspection on another airplane. I could have picked one of seven other FAC's to go to Nha Trang, but I wanted to go to 21st TASS to make sure my orders for my next assignment were properly cut, so they'd coincide with my plans to meet my wife and son in Hawaii on July 10, then on by ship to Frisco to pick up my new VW. I wound up the evening writing to my wife on a dining table in the Nha Trang Officers' Club, with the girls cleaning up the place around me before they went home.

My Year in Viet Nam

Figure 18.1
Air Force Flight Nurse " Charlie Brown" joins us for a party

Figure 18.2
Nha Trang

A notable fact about Nha Trang--in consonance with the Buddhist religion so widely practiced in Viet Nam, there was a huge statue of a seated Buddha on a hillside just a short distance North of the town. It convinced me that Buddha was indeed revered.

The airplane wasn't ready until Saturday afternoon, so I had a mini-vacation. I spent most of it reading and napping, although I " worked in" getting typhoid and typhus shots.

My replacement was supposed to already be " in country", so he surely would show up on time. Two more FAC's were scheduled to arrive ahead of him. That was a far cry from when I first arrived, when I waited two months for additional pilots.

The Sunday evening movie started out interesting, but my attention was interrupted by misdirected bombs on friendly troops. Bombs come from the air, right? That was bound to be in my bailiwick, so I flew an hour to try to sort that out. By the time I landed it was an hour after sunset. That's pretty dark, with no moon, in that part of the world.

Monday turned out to be a busy day, finding out where the bombs of the night before came from, etc. They fell near some friendly soldiers, and a few were slightly injured, none seriously hurt or killed, but scared!?! The slip-up turned out to be in that all-important link, communications. A mistake was made in encoding, transmitting, or decoding, a message.

On Tuesday evening, the 9th, we had a bit of excitement in Qui Nhon. A little after dark, some refugees were playing cards in one of the miserable shacks just off the end of the runway, by kerosene lamp light. A disagreement came up, resulting in a scuffle, during which the lamp was knocked over and started a fire, to which the Qui Nhon Fire Department responded in full force.

On the North side of the street connecting Route 19 to the docks on the causeway, there were two large civilian petroleum storage tanks, a short distance from the shore, guarded by a Vietnamese and an American. While all the excitement was

My Year in Viet Nam

Figure 18.3
 After the Fire, Center Left; Commercial Terminal, Upper Center

Figure 18.4
 After the Oil Storage Tank Fire

going on at the end of the runway, two or more Viet Cong members walked from the West past the airfield, and turned in at the gate to the storage tank area. They shot and killed one guard, and wounded the other. They then set timed, plastic explosive charges against the bases of the tanks, and walked out of the enclosure, returning the way they had come. The charges went off, we heard the explosions from our quarters, we went out and looked. There was a huge fire about three blocks from us. I took pictures from my front door.

The Fire Department had gotten the fire out at the end of the runway, but now they really had their hands full, and spent a busy night. The tanks were still smoking when I went up to fly on Wednesday morning.

At first it was thought that the fire in the shabby shack housing area was started purposely as a diversion to cover the attack on the oil storage tanks, but it turned out to have been just a coincidence.

The Province Chief's police force was pretty good. Within a few days they identified and arrested the perpetrators of the murder and the big tank fire.

CHAPTER XIX

ILLNESS

We also got some not-so-good news on Wednesday. Phil Jones looked in the mirror, and thought his eyes looked yellow. He asked his room mate if he thought they looked yellow, he said they did, so Phil went on sick call. They looked yellow to the Flight Surgeon, so he ordered a bunch of tests. Diagnosis: Hepatitis. Prognosis: to the hospital at Cam Ranh Bay or Tokyo, two to three months full bed rest.

Phil and his wife, married less than two years, with a baby daughter, had been planning R & R in Hawaii in June. That disruption of plans was worse than being shot down (which hadn't lasted too long). Phil was transported to Cam Ranh Bay hospital.

Thursday night we were entertained by another USO troupe, a male MC, and two ladies, in their mid-thirties, I guessed. One played an accordion, the other a bass viol. Most of their numbers were fast and loud, e. g. *Beer Barrel Polka*. The accordionist, especially, was drenched in perspiration--it was a very warm evening. Everyone had a good time, anyway.

I couldn't guess how much salary these relatively unknown entertainers were paid, but there surely must have been easier places and more pleasant surroundings in which to make a living. Perhaps it was a spirit of adventure, a desire to travel, an opportunity to gain experience, but I liked to think they were a bit patriotic, and wanted to provide a little cheer in the lives of these men and women so far from home.

The FAC shuffle continued. On May 12 I got word that three of my FAC's were being transferred to other assignments. With Phil going to the hospital, that was a loss of four in one day. But two new ones, both Majors, were coming in. We were still the premier FAC trainers in Viet Nam, it appeared. Lt. Col. Hennis, my replacement, was due in before long. I hoped that I'd be able to get him properly checked out in the job before I left, and give him the benefit of all the things I'd learned in almost a year, thinking I'd leave the operation in better condition than I found it in. At least he shouldn't have all the same problems I'd had.

The heat was with us again. I had to climb to about 5,000 feet to find 70 degrees. Lower than that, the cross ventilation provided by open windows and open flying suit sleeves deployed in the slip stream, was my air conditioning.

The fan from home was once more a tremendous blessing When the power was on I could set it to blow the full length of the bed all night long, and sleep well.

Gib said he'd seen some of the new Lt. Cols. coming in to our ALO jobs, including Wes Hennis, who was destined to replace me. He said they all were old gray-haired men. Some more pilots were being called back from Code 3C. I had avoided Code 1C by volunteering for a flying job. I guessed it was better I did it when I did, rather than waiting.

Sunday night, the 14th, we had another beer and steak party at the flight line, honoring a FAC who had been flying in support of the ROK Capital Infantry Division; his year was complete, and he was headed home.

During the evening, some of my FAC's began calling me "the Old Man". It was meant as a compliment, and I felt honored. Of course I *was* the oldest of the team.

It was traditional to call a military commander " the Old Man." It was just one more extension of the respect I seemed to enjoy from those I supervised. It made me feel good about my relationship with them, and validated my theories about supervision. My basic theory was that everyone wanted to do well, and do the right thing in his job. The supervisor's place was to guide the person supervised in the best way to get his tasks done, and to show him his efforts were appreciated. If the proper relationships and attitudes were established, there was seldom any need for " chewing the man out". There were better corrective methods than showing anger, anyway.

On Monday, a little good news from Phil Jones--he called

to say his doctor at Cam Ranh Bay told him he might be able to leave the hospital there and come back to Qui Nhon in as little as two weeks. Phil said, emphatically,

" Don't give my bed away!"

Tuesday morning I flew with one of my two newest FAC's, Dan Wall, for his familiarization ride. When he was trained, I'd assign him to Tuy Hoa.

Here I was, Day 312 of my year, May 17, only 54 more to go, to USA soil once more. I could almost hold my breath that long. But I'd better get busy, several Letters of Evaluation, Officer Effectiveness Reports, and an End of Tour Report to write, plus no noticeable slacking off in my flying. The flying was the part I liked best, anyway. I did manage to make my Wednesday scheduled visit to Tuy Hoa, and flew Visual Reconnaissance on the way back.

On Thursday I received a surprise package from Smith Ladies' Aid, the group my wife's Mother belonged to. They sent a towel, wash cloth, soap, chewing gum, licorice, Kleenex, Kool Aid, and stationery. Shades of World War II! Weren't the Ladies Lovely?! God Bless 'em all!

Friday morning I was up early to fly with one of my new FAC's in the front seat. The mission was to put in two air strikes on an unoccupied (nothing and no people) open area in preparation for an " insertion" (helicopter landing) of a Green Beret force.

May 19 was Ho Chi Minh's Birthday, but we didn't celebrate.

May 23 was a HOT one, Wes Hennis had arrived, and I took him with me, in the back seat, on a three hour VR mission. Even at 5500 feet it was well above 70 degrees. Wes' helmet didn't have a visor, so I couldn't open my windows for better cross ventilation. When we got back I was weak and had a headache from the heat and perspiring so much. Three aspirins plus lots of liquids and taking it easy for a while fixed me all up.

I discovered that all the old Lt. Cols., except Gibson and Mueller, looked older to me than I did. Wes was almost a year and a half younger than I, but the little hair he had left was totally gray. Exigencies of the service--having to put the old timers out front! Interesting sidelight--Wes had come from flying C-141's!

May 23 was Buddha's Birthday, widely celebrated, and much more important in South Viet Nam than Ho Chi Minh's. It was as much celebrated as Christmas is in America, even with displays much like our Christmas Nativity Scenes. In honor of the Holiday, there was a truce, no one was supposed to do any shooting. I wore my flak vest just the same. I didn't need any holes in my hide. The vest was made of half-inch thick nylon, it surely did keep the heat in.

On my Tuesday trip to Cheo Reo I brought my newest and youngest FAC, Jack Morris, back with me. My senior FAC there, Dick Smith, was concerned about Jack's lack of experience. Jack had been out of flying school only about six months. I wasn't really greatly concerned. Six months out of flying school in the forties found me and a lot of contemporaries flying bombers and fighters pretty proficiently. So I planned to fly with him a few times to build his self-confidence, and knew he'd do well.

We stopped in at Pleiku, and found the weather there pleasantly cool. It wasn't even too bad in Qui Nhon.

Phil Jones came back from the hospital on Friday, the 26th, directed to loaf for at least two weeks, on a diet of all he could eat and no alcoholic beverages for at least six months. For having had hepatitis he was really making a fast recovery.

Dave Ward came up with a tremendous case of hives. He was grounded and given a ten day supply of antihistamines. All symptoms went away after about four days, so he got back on flying status and stopped the medicine. 24 hours later the hives were back in full force!

On Sunday I deviated from my " day off" and flew more than three hours with Jack Morris. I concluded he'd been well

My Year in Viet Nam

Figure 19.1
    Celebrating Buddha's Birhday, ARVN Post

Figure 19.2
    Cheo Reo Base

213

trained in flying school, and would get along fine in this new job. I also concluded that I liked flight instructing! Of course I did some of it with each newly assigned FAC.

I got up early Monday morning, May 29, to go to the MARS station to call my older son and congratulate him on his graduation from High School. When I reached for my shirt, I got a bad kink in my back (nothing that had not happened before). I struggled into my clothes and managed to drive to the MARS Station. But they couldn't get through on the radio.

I went back to quarters and lay down, took aspirin and muscle relaxant pills, but nothing helped the back pain, it just got worse. I might have to go to the hospital and be put in traction.

Adding gin (several drinks) to my self-prescribed treatment Monday evening and Tuesday didn't cure the sore back. The Flight Surgeon was himself hospitalized at Cam Ranh Bay, so I couldn't see him.

I finally got to see an Army Flight Surgeon on Wednesday morning. He prescribed rest on a hard bed, and Miltown tranquilizers, two pills every six hours, continuing the aspirin. He said Miltown was a better muscle relaxant than Robaxin, which I had taken in the past. After four Miltowns I was so relaxed I was almost melting into the bed, so I decided to decrease the dosage to one pill. I had already spent 40 out of 48 hours in bed, but I was getting better.

I probably would have been better off getting right back into bed on Monday morning, instead of trying to make that MARS call, which didn't go through, anyway.

We must have had everything pretty well organized, or I had very competent help. The whole 22nd Division FAC/ALO system seemed to get along fine with me in bed. Perhaps the worst part of the ordeal was the temperature, going over 100 degrees every day. That little fan from home was a life-saver.

Sympathy is universal. When I finally got to the Mess Hall on Thursday morning, one of the girl attendants asked me very solicitously,

" Trung-ta seeck?"

Figure 19.3
    Tuy Hoa, Town, Air Field, (PSP Runway), Mountain

Figure 19.4
    New Tuy Hoa Fighter Base

I explained as best I could that my back hurt, and she looked very concerned.

And Mama-san had been completely noiseless around the place when she thought I was asleep.

I couldn't feel too sorry for myself when I frequently saw such things as a little girl picking at scabs the size of half dollars, on her scabies-infected scalp. Surely many little tykes must have died of infections.

I'd never heard of dying from a sore back.

CHAPTER XX

TERRORISM, VIET CONG STYLE

The June 2 issue of STARS AND STRIPES had a sad story to tell.

The account told of Father Matthieu, whose family name was Nguyen Van Nghi. He had been a Chaplain at the Vietnamese Army camp in Nha Trang, and then in 1964 was assigned by his bishop to be the Catholic pastor of the little village of Phong Dien.

When he arrived there, it was just a cluster of weather beaten shacks. From this meager beginning, Father Matthieu developed the refugee camp into a model village embodying many of the characteristics of a large city.

Together with the villagers, he laid out the houses in blocks, and lined the blocks with cypress and eucalyptus trees among the sharply defined intersections of sandy roads. He saw to it that each house had its own small fence and gateway.

Later, when he built his church and an intermediate school, he allowed for a plaza between them. He used no blueprints, but developed the plans in his mind, and built the village as he went. He acquired materials and funds for the refugee center through the Vietnamese government, through benefactors in the United States, and from his friends in the US 4th Marine Regiment, based nearby. He organized the village, and taught the people to be clean and polite.

Since many of the people had fled from Viet Cong controlled areas, and had no way to make a living, he taught them trades. He taught the women to sew, and to weave conical straw hats for market. He built and equipped a barber shop, where the older men could earn a wage, and the younger ones could learn the business.

He organized a laundry business to serve the nearby Marines, and for those mechanically inclined, he opened a bicycle repair shop.

Father Matthieu believed that the future of his country

rested in the hands of his children, and he spared nothing to ensure their education. He opened a nursery, a primary school and a middle school, and had plans for a high school.

He saw to it that orphans were cared for, and taught the children to dance and sing.

When the 4th Marine Regiment moved into the area, Father Matthieu became a popular figure around the command post. He obtained medicine and medical supplies for his village from the regimental field hospital. He arranged weekly visits to his village by Navy Surgeon, Ted Gross.

" Father Matthieu was an unforgettable person," said Gross. " He was always trying to do something more for his people. He never wanted anything for himself--it was always for them. He was a fantastic person in what he accomplished for his village. He was a very aggressive person, but in a very subtle way. His cause was so just, that it was almost impossible to refuse him anything," Gross said.

The 4th Marines helped Father build the schools, the barbershop, and the laundry business. They donated tin, concrete, and building materials to the village.

" The villagers had a tremendous respect for him," said Gross. " He was an outstanding example of what the Church was doing in this country."

Father Matthieu and the doctor used to joke in private about the Viet Cong. They would never harm him, he felt, for he had never done any harm to them.

But the Viet Cong did come.

They came to the village of Phong Dien. They came in force. They came to murder the Catholic pastor of Phong Dien.

During the early morning darkness, they stole into the village and surrounded his church. They told him to open his door and come outside. When he refused, they poured high explosive rounds through the walls of his rectory.

Father Matthieu fell, wounded by a piece of shrapnel. Just as the Viet Cong broke into the rectory, mortar fire from the nearby Marines drove them off.

Father Matthieu crawled almost 100 meters to the Nuns'

quarters, where the Marine reactionary force found him.

He was treated and flown by Marine helicopter to the medical station at Phu Bai. There, Father Matthieu, Vietnamese Catholic priest, died of his wounds.

Now the church was being repaired by the villagers and the Marines of the 4th Regiment. Father's little city still stood-- a tribute to a priest who gave his life for the people of Viet Nam.

The blood of martyrs still flowed.

Figure 20.1
    A Montagnard Town, Pattern for Father Matthieu's Little Village, Phong Dien

CHAPTER XXI

END OF TOUR REPORT

I was obligated by 504th Tactical Air Support Group Regulation to submit a report at the end of my tour, recording my activities, my problems, and my recommendations. It ended up being six pages long, getting quite detailed in some areas. I started working on it in mid-June, and finally sent it in just before leaving for home. The following is a summary of the finally submitted report.

I began by saying that this had been a very interesting and personally rewarding tour. The work was continually challenging, never routine or boring.

Very real progress in both civil and military terms had been made in the 22nd Division Tactical Area. A year earlier the rural areas were under Viet Cong control, and North Vietnamese Army units moved around at will. Now government control had been reestablished in the major population areas, and real progress at pacification was being made. The combination of ground forces and tactical air support had thrown the Viet Cong and the NVA almost entirely on the defensive.

Problem areas in the beginning were:
Not enough Forward Air Controllers
Lack of knowledge of the tactical air support system
Failure of communication, due to language differences,
> i. e. Vietnamese, Korean and English used in the same area, failures to convey exact meanings were almost inevitable.
> Lack of suitable radios; Vietnamese forces were not equipped with needed radios.
> Radio failures
> Failure of people to properly use radios to communicate

Lack of coordination among users of tactical air.

Further problems

My Year in Viet Nam

Poor target selection
Some requested targets had no tactical value
Some targets requested were backups, " in pocket" just in case a more significant target showed up
In many cases artillery was available to Free World Forces and would have been more effective.
Ineffective use of FAC's' Visual Reconnaissance by their assigned units; real time observations were discounted or ignored by Free World forces to which FAC's were assigned, and seldom resulted in strike requests
FAC's were frequently handicapped by lack of target knowledge because they had not seen the target area ahead of time
Overlapping Areas of Operation
Lack of clear directives on how to request, clear and coordinate air strikes
Shortage of FAC aircraft, well known, help was supposed to be on the way
Instructional time for FAC check out was being logged as copilot time because ALO's and experienced FAC's were not deemed qualified as Instructors. The ALO or a Senior FAC was in fact in command of such flights, and responsible for assuring that the new pilot could navigate in the environment, identify targets and deal with crosswinds and other conditions peculiar to the area, like short runways It was a distortion of fact to log copilot time.

There were good things to report, too. Everyone involved in the system had a strong drive to get the job done right. The FAC's of all units, the Army L-19 pilots, and all the Advisory teams on the ground worked well and enthusiastically together. Maintenance personnel worked long hard hours in conditions ranging from difficult to impossible, and kept the airplanes serviced and flyable.

Some things that needed to be done:

Obtain better radios

Improve knowledge and understanding of the tactical air support system

Any entity authorized to request air strikes should be thoroughly and frequently retrained in viable target selection

I made numerous other recommendations, but two that I considered vital were free exchange of Visual Reconnaissance sightings, with greater use of them in target selection, and coordination of all air strikes in II Corps through a single agency, II DASC. Requests by TACC/DASC at 7th Air Force should funnel through II DASC, so that everyone would be working together.

I made some other observations:

There was no noticeable difference in capability between FAC's who came from Tactical Fighter backgrounds and those who did not.

The apparent assumption of training units in the US that Tactical Air Support operates in a totally hostile environment was not valid in Viet Nam, and probably would not be so in future operations.

Figure 21.1
 Herb 01's Night Time Headquarters, Best Pillow Case in Viet Nam, September 1, 1966 to July 7, 1967

CHAPTER XXII

MISCELLANY

There were situations, activities and events that have not been reported in this account up to this point, but just the same affected our operations, or at least aroused our curiosity and concerns.

One of the puzzles to me early on was where the Viet Cong got all the explosive materials they used for land mines they used along the main roads, and the lesser routes connecting the hamlets. I got a clue one day when I spotted a quite obvious foot trail, many tracks leading across several paddies, ending at an unexploded 500 pound bomb. Obviously it had been hand-carried, during the night before, by the Viet Cong toward a secure area for disassembly. When daylight came, it was left there for retrieval the next night. There was an ARVN APC unit nearby, so I called their American Advisor on the radio and reported what I'd seen. He said they'd take care of it. So, they blew it up, making quite a hole in the farmer's paddy, I suppose.

Attached to the 22nd Advisory Group was a young US Marine Lieutenant. He was always trying to work a scheme to get the US Navy involved in our operations. His big dream was to get a battleship sitting off shore to hurl huge shells at targets. We didn't really have any targets justifying the use of such armament. A scheme was finally worked out to involve a submarine in an intelligence gathering operation.

There was a relatively uninhabited sandy beach area along the shore North of Qui Nhon, with known VC operations in the area back of the beach. So, a plan was worked out to have the submarine standing off shore, while we would put in an air strike by A-1's on the beach area, then launch a rubber raft from the sub to gather intelligence information. I directed the air strike on what appeared to be some fox holes in the sandy beach area, then the landing team boarded their rubber raft and rowed to shore. They apprehended two suspects who had survived the bombardment and began questioning them about likely buddies back up in the hills above the beach. The two refused to talk, so they were blindfolded and led up and down the beach in opposite directions. When they were a couple hundred yards apart, a shot was fired at the point where they had started. Each prisoner was told,

"Your buddy wouldn't talk, so we just shot and killed him. If you don't answer our questions, you will get the same treatment."

Both began telling all about their buddies back on the hillsides.

The operation was successful.

I was flying along the coast one day when I got a radio call.

"FAC over the coast North of Qui Nhon, this is Navy Destroyer about a half mile off the coast, we'd like you to spot some artillery rounds for us."

"What coordinates will you be firing at?"

They gave me a set of coordinates, and there were no friendly people or structures anywhere near it, only a rocky hillside with some scrawny brush on it.

"OK, fire when you're ready."

I saw the flash from the gun muzzle, but did not see any ground impact in the target area. I reported no splash. They tried about three or four more times, but I never did see where their rounds were hitting. Maybe they were firing blanks.

During my first several months at Qui Nhon, a hamlet area some miles up the coast just didn't look right. The dirt in some places didn't match the surrounding surfaces. I concluded that the VC were digging tunnels and spreading the dirt around on the top of the ground. When the Monsoon came, they were given away, my suspicions were confirmed. There were extensive cave-ins, revealing where the tunnels had been. That same thing had happened in the area of Operation Irving.

Two big holes in the ground intrigued me. One was

Southeast of English Field, perhaps a half mile from the Bong Son River, downstream from the Highway 1 and railroad bridges. The other was a little distance West of Highway 1, some miles South of the Bong Son. Both were in populated areas, not far from houses. The openings were at least ten feet across, and it was dark down inside of them. I guessed they might have been access to extensive underground works. I never saw anyone on the edges of the openings.

The highway bridge across the Bong Son had long since been destroyed, so that when our convoys went to English, they crossed the river on the railroad bridge.

The First US Air Cavalry, as noted in earlier Chapters, played an active part in combatting the Communist forces. Their more or less permanent base was located at An Khe, on the North side of Highway 19, just at the foot of the higher hills as one approached the Central Plateau. Their site was clearly identified by a very large painting of their shoulder patch, a black horse's head inside a yellow shield, on the East side of the high hill just West of the encampment. There was no mistaking their base for anyone else's. Besides the normal buildings and tent sites, there was a good runway for cargo aircraft, with revetments for visitors, and a large number of helicopter pads for their UH-1's (Hueys). Part way through my tour, they began building a new runway parallel to the first. Surrounding the base was a security barrier of four high barbed wire fences.

Their security measures were not always successful in warding off attack. One night the Viet Cong managed to set up a large number of mortars not far from the base, and all began firing their shells at the same time. Scores of helicopters were damaged or destroyed. By the time the reaction forces got to the mortar sites, the mortars and their operators had melted away.

Cavalry operational units were deployed to other sites in the Province, and supported mostly by air. Heavy lift helicopters moved fuel bladders, ammunition, etc., while Hueys moved the people.

One such deployment was to English. There was a hill

adjacent to the Southeast end of the runway. Fuel bladders were flown in and set up on the top of the hill, and the ammunition dump was established at the base of the hill. Two Mohawk reconnaissance aircraft were parked just off the end of the runway, not far from the ammo dump.

The Cav force encamped there did not want to be sneaked up on in the darkness, so periodically during the night they fired an artillery launched flare so they could look around the area for any intruders. One of the flares was still burning when it struck the ground, in the fuel dump. It ignited one or more fuel bladders, and burning fuel ran down the hill into the ammo dump, starting a fire there, which began setting off the artillery shells and other explosives. The two aircraft were riddled, and shell fragments even rained down on the metal roof of the dug in shelter of the local ARVN Commander, near the other end of the runway. He thought his post was under attack. The ARVN's assigned FAC for that unit, (one of ours), not knowing any of what had been going on, made his routine call prior to landing the next morning, and was told,

" Don't land here! We have shrapnel flying all over the place!"

He finally was able to land safely, later in the morning, and found out what had been going on.

I had flown over the upper An Lao and Bong Son valleys, and had seen what looked like wooden barracks, among other things, relative to military operations. I reported it to the Intelligence folks at Ba Gi, but there wasn't much we could do about it, we had no operations going on there at the time. Later on, I wondered if the information had been passed on to others, when I saw a missile launching ship off the coast opposite English. It was firing salvos of missiles whose targets I could not see, they were so far inland. I wasn't able to establish communications with the ship, so never did find out what was really going on.

I had misgivings about the usefulness, effectiveness or suitability of using B-52's to bomb in South Viet Nam. A camera was sent to me to take pictures of an area of a suspected trail in a remote section of Binh Dinh Province, which had been bombed a couple of days earlier. There were foot trails into and out of the craters, as if foot traffic had slowed very little. But a sad event convinced me that B-52's had limited if any justified usefulness.

A detachment of the 22nd Advisory Team went to see the results of a B-52 strike, and came back with sad news of what the strike had done to a school, during school hours, injuring and killing children. What could the team say to the poor parents? The bombs had missed the intended target by quite some distance.

On the other hand, the bombing of the Phu Cats by B-52's in preparation for Operation Irving had been helpful to us.

Already described were the typical hamlets near Qui Nhon--no particular street pattern, the appearance that the houses had been built along already existing trails, so that the streets seemed to wander in any direction.

The Montagnard villages in the " back country" around Pleiku were quite different. They were laid out with parallel streets, in a rectangular pattern, as if there had been some planning.

I wondered if US Army pilots received any judgment training in their schooling. I saw an LOH (Loach) helicopter one day making repeated very low firing passes at a " hooch" in an apparently abandoned area, setting themselves up as an easy target for ground fire. Another time a Huey was chasing a black pajama clad man I thought to be a farmer across the paddies. They would have been sitting ducks for any VC in the cover surrounding the area, and they surely did not improve our image with the Vietnamese.

Another time, flying up the coast North of Tuy Hoa, I heard a loud explosion, then another. I finally located the source. An Army O-1 was circling a hamlet below, firing rocket propelled grenades at some imagined target. There was no visible target that would make the risks of low flying and possible return fire worth taking.

As noted elsewhere, the ROK's used a very sophisticated(?) method to clear the Viet Cong out of an area.

They simply moved all the normal residents out, then assumed that anyone still there was Viet Cong, to be dealt with accordingly.

When they were assigned a new tactical area, they moved in and established a comfortable camp and defensive positions, and set up a religious center located in the middle of the area. When that was all done, they would go looking for the " bad guys". On patrol, they were noted for using very little ammunition. They would set up positions along a trail and wait for enemy troops to come by. Unless they were substantially outnumbered, they did not fire their weapons, but would take their opponents out using karate or other hand combat methods. They were justifiably feared by the Viet Cong.

Along the road to Ba Gi were brick making facilities. The bricks were formed from clay mixed with rice straw to hold them together, then fired in small kilns.

At another location along the road to Ba Gi was a primitive stone quarry. The stones were dug out, then broken into smaller pieces, using heavy malls. Of course, their production capacity was quite limited.

When the construction of the new Phu Cat runway began, a new and bigger quarry, with a regular rock crusher, was put to use. And a section of the railroad was repaired and pressed into service to haul the crushed stone to the runway building site. That was the only train I saw in operation in my year in Viet Nam.

Then there was the saga of the Jeeps. We had run short, so I had one brought over by C-123 from Cheo Reo, where we had an extra. But we were still charged with more than we had, at Qui Nhon. We located one being used by the ROK ALO, but he refused to return it, so we got it charged out to him. Nevertheless, we were still short one Jeep, and could not account for it. I finally concluded it must have been dropped in the harbor when they were being unloaded some years before. It continued to be a matter for correspondence even after I left for home. Wes Hennis did not sign for it.

CHAPTER XXIII

FINISHING THE TOUR

At the Geneva Conference in 1954, the group of world powers established a division of Viet Nam into North and South, with a DMZ (Demilitarized Zone) between them, approximately along the 17th Parallel. An International Control Commission was formed to keep track of military movements, supply movements, etc., in both North and South Viet Nam. It was still in existence in 1966 and 1967. The Commission consisted of Indian, Canadian and Polish Army Officers. It was difficult to tell if they had any effect on what the opposing forces were doing. The Commission maintained field groups at various locations throughout the divided country.

One of the stations was in Qui Nhon. Members rotated from one station to another on a fairly frequent basis. On June 2, Captain Harold Decost, the Canadian member, whom we had gotten to know over the previous six weeks, hosted a cocktail party to tell us goodbye, and to introduce his successor, Major Richards.

At the party, I met and talked quite a while with a Vietnamese Army Dai-uy (Captain) and his wife, and daughter. They were fascinating. He joined the army in 1952 (against the French, probably), and they had been married since 1954. The oldest of their three children was the daughter, just 12. They spent 2000 piastres a month to send her to a Catholic private school in Saigon. The husband spoke Vietnamese, French and English, the wife spoke Vietnamese, Malay, Cantonese and English. She told me that many Vietnamese children did not go to school because their parents could not afford it. When it came to a choice between food and school, food won out.

My judgment was that the private school in Saigon was well worth what they were paying. I had a lengthy conversation with the 12-year old. She spoke very good English, as well as French and Vietnamese. I was amazed at how much she knew about the world and international affairs. She was more knowledgable about what was going on in the world than any graduating High School Senior I knew in the USA, including my own son.

The wife told me of a 14-year-old boy who supported his widowed mother and six younger children by fishing. He kept his ten year old brother at home to help repair nets, etc. Some days he made 400 piastres, on an exceptional day he might make 700. That was from less than US $4 to just under US $6 a day.

Also she told me that by Vietnamese custom, a woman whose husband dies may not remarry. The longer she is a widow, the more highly she is regarded. I asked the lady if that might not be a sad and lonely life, not having a husband. She said that if the widow did remarry, her former husband's family would come and take away all her children by him. She did not know the reason for these customs.

May ended with only 62:45 logged. So there, Gib. June started off slowly, too.

By Saturday night, June 3, my back was feeling well enough to attend a cocktail party, with Wes Hennis, hosted by Lt. Col. Rutherford, (noted earlier), CO of the 37th Combat Support Group. It was a small outfit, serving Air Force Transportation units. Only a small group attended, fifteen or so.

On Sunday, my back was enough better to fly an airplane to Nha Trang for inspection, with a further objective of making sure that my orders for travel back to the States were being properly cut, and to check on all the things I had to do to finish off my obligations, turn in reports, equipment, and so on. When it was time to go, I wanted to be ready.

Transportation assured me they could get me on my way to Honolulu on July 10. The only medical obligation was to get the skin test for T. B., some time between 6 and 30 days before my departure.

Both my FAC's and the airplane at Cheo Reo were gone for the moment, so, on Tuesday, Hilliard and I flew over to the far side of that Province to direct air strikes. It took an hour and a half to return, and we landed back in Qui Nhon an hour after sunset. It was pretty darn DARK! Flare pots were runway lights again.

Earlier in the day, we'd had other friendlies trying to bomb Binh Dinh Province's soldiers, and a quartet of helicopters shooting at a group of ARVN soldiers with American Advisors. We managed to get those activities stopped before anyone got hurt. Sometimes we did earn our pay.

Flying went along about as usual for the next several days, with me accumulating hours at a slower rate. By mid-month I had only about 20 hours. Wes was gaining experience and getting well checked out. We got word that Dave Griffin would be going to Pleiku to become II Corps FAC, Scroggin's and Gibson's old job, after returning from R & R, in July. We were still turning out capable, well trained men. His replacement at Qui Nhon, Frank Herron, arrived on June 13, in plenty of time to get worked into his new position by the time Dave left.

I was invited to 22nd Division Headquarters for a Change of Command ceremony on June 14. The Engineer Battalion was getting a new Commander. I felt the invitation was really for the Air Force, to be represented by me.

Work was not going away, I still had five OER's to write and an End of Tour Report to turn in, before July 10.

Well, there was almost a paper storm, getting those OER's written. I had to get them all ready for Col. Gibson's endorsements. He was due at Nha Trang in his clearing process to go home, on June 16, so I had to make a quick trip to have the last ones there, that day, for his review, comments and signatures.

It was so hot in quarters Thursday night that when the power (and the fans) went off, we fled to the outdoors. The slight breeze off the water helped somewhat.

A new day dawned! The plumbing crew came and did its thing, and everyone in our wing of Quarters finally had hot water! And there weren't any little red worms in it, either! I was being gently prepared for return to civilization.

More reason to celebrate:

That Sunday, June 18, 1967, was not only important to me as Fathers' Day, but because of two anniversaries, Mom's and Dad's 48th Wedding Anniversary, and the 25th Anniversary

Figure 23.1
FAC Gathering at Qui Nhon, July, 1967. Front Row, Left to Right: Jones, Hennis. Welch, Pritchett, Griffin

Figure 23.2
A Last Good Look at Qui Nhon

of my being sworn into the Army.

A Major whom we all knew, assigned to the Army Advisory Team at Qui Nhon, was a passenger on an airplane which crashed on landing at An Khe late Saturday night. He was not among the survivors, so he was declared missing until the bodies of the deceased could be identified. We mourned him and all the others.

On Sunday and Monday we had a visitor from the 504th Group. He was Chief of the Standardization Board. He flew with one of our pilots, and asked a lot of questions. He didn't criticize our operation, so it must have met the Standards. I told him nothing he could say would hurt my feelings, since I would leave in about three weeks, and he couldn't blame anything on Wes Hennis yet.

On Wednesday Wes and I and several others went to Pleiku for a conference. Ordinarily Wes and I would have flown an O-1, but we had none to spare, so we rode in a Huey, along with the Army Advisors. The ride in the "chopper" was o. k., but the durn thing shook all the time. I preferred airplanes.

Wes' and my trip to Saigon for a conference at MACV on Saturday went well enough, but it lasted longer than we expected, and the weather was bad, so we stayed over night. We bunked at a leased hotel, the Mekong, about six blocks from the Rex, where the Officers' Club was. I saw AFIT classmate Bill Thurman, who had spent the first half of his SEA year flying "Thuds" (F-105's) out of Thailand, and was now assigned to 7th Air Force Headquarters. On the way out of the Rex I saw George Evans, from my last days in SAC at Sheppard, now assigned to MACV. Either it was a small world, or all the Air Force was taking its turn.

Traffic was so congested in Saigon that we didn't get off at Tan Son Nhut next morning until ten o'clock, and we had to stop at Nha Trang to get the radio compass repaired. It was past 1730, dark again, when we arrived back at Qui Nhon. So ended a busy two days of good training for Wes.

My back started to hurt again, so I took a couple more Miltowns and went to bed.

My Year in Viet Nam

I had been trying to get my End of Tour Report written, and on Sunday rewrote it for the third time. I still was not satisfied with it, but just might turn it in the way it was. I planned to keep a copy, mostly for my own entertainment.

The evening of June 26 I flew out to the 41st Regiment Headquarters for a steak fry to honor their Senior US Army Advisor, Major Eitel, who was scheduled to leave for home on July 2. There was a party for him the next evening by the Division Advisors, and he was to depart for Saigon the next morning. Yes, we all were also getting our turns to go home, too.

With less than two weeks to go, I began sorting things out--things to mail home, stuff to go in hold baggage, items to hand carry, equipment to turn in, and things to give or throw away. I also started through the clearing process, to be sure I was meeting all my obligations. And I was still flying. I got more than five hours June 28 and 29, and finished the month with 50:05.

On Thursday afternoon, I packed up all my issued gear not needed for flying, and took it to Nha Trang to turn it in. I also took an airplane for an inspection, and got that T. B. skin test.

My new planned date for final departure from Qui Nhon was July 7. I would finish processing out of the 21st TASS, and spend that night, at Nha Trang, then the next night at Ton Son Nhut, before getting on my flight to Hawaii on the ninth.

I did my letter writing on the 29th at the 21st TASS Orderly Room. Also writing personal letters, with a typewriter, at another desk, was Lt. Col. Willard Barnett, the new Squadron CO, replacing Dick Ransbottom. Barney, as we called him, flew an occasional O-1 directed air strike against the VC holed up in the hills West of Nha Trang. They were never very far away, it seemed, anywhere in South Viet Nam.

Friday I spent processing and waiting for the airplane, and got my "Ticket" for my flight out of Ton Son Nhut. It was to make one stop, on Guam.

On Saturday afternoon, July 1, I flew back to Qui Nhon. Bob Smith had just returned from R & R, and rode with me.

Sunday afternoon I mailed a last package home, then flew madly off to Cheo Reo, where I was invited for a steak dinner that evening. I flew VR over the old familiar route back to Qui Nhon on Monday, and got confirmation of my flight leaving Ton Son Nhut, with a stop in Guam, to arrive in Honolulu early on the tenth, just as planned for many months. On the 4th of July, I flew to Tuy Hoa for lunch, my last visit there. On the way back, I spent some time just kind of cruising, saying goodbye to the general area I had grown so familiar with, and even grown to love.

Wednesday night there was a little get together for me in the gazebo on the beach. That gave everybody all of Thursday to recover before seeing me off on Friday morning. It was great to see good friends, and a little sad that it was for perhaps the last time, for most of them.

Somewhere in all that activity, I was asked to report to Division Headquarters. Col. Hieu pinned a Vietnamese medal on me, expressed regret that I was leaving, and thanked me for having been helpful to the 22nd ARVN and to the people of Viet Nam. He seemed surprised that I was leaving so soon. I expressed my thanks for having been able to help, my pride in having served with the 22nd ARVN, and my admiration for the people of Viet Nam.

Of course the job wasn't done yet, but I was leaving it in good hands, all the FAC's I'd flown and worked with, the maintenance men, the men in the radio room, the Intelligence Clerk, and all the 22nd Division Advisory team. I felt the FAC/ALO operation was much improved since my arrival, thanks to all of them. And I was optimistic about the future of Viet Nam. I was also pleased that Wes Hennis had picked up the job so readily, and confident he'd do it well.

I was also sure Mama-san would continue to look after her charges in an exemplary manner, and Tanh would continue saluting.

My hold baggage was packed on Wednesday, and picked up on Thursday. Friday morning I stowed my carry along baggage behind the back seat of an O-1, and Wes flew me to Nha Trang, where we wished each other the best, and he flew back to work, as Herb 01.

That last flight brought me to 7:15 for the month of July, and a total of 823:20 in the Bird Dog.

I turned in the rest of my flying gear and completed my other obligations. When the Supply clerks came to my white helmet, they took one sniff and threw it in the trash can. I could only agree that no one else would be able to stand the smell.

The next day I got a ride in a Gooney Bird to Ton Son Nhut, the busiest airport in the world, and spent one last night there. The next afternoon I checked in at the Commercial Terminal for my flight that evening, the ninth, and watched in amazement as rats ran in and out of holes in the cushions of the chairs and couches in the waiting room.

Perhaps it was a parallel of the Viet Cong still running in and out of their jungle hiding areas.

The flight was on time, and we made our scheduled stop at Anderson AFB, on Guam. A lot of building had been done since my stay there in 1955. I arrived in Honolulu on the morning of July 10. Customs wanted to know what was in the package I had for Msgr. Feiten, and I couldn't tell them. So we opened it, and found a beautiful summer weight set of vestments for saying Catholic Mass. There was no duty on that!

That evening brought a joyous reunion with my wife, Alberta, and our son, Carl. After a few days on Oahu, we boarded the S. S. Lurline, a Matson Liner, for the trip to Frisco. Since I'd had a trip across the Atlantic on another Matson Liner, the S. S. Mariposa, in 1945, returning from my B-17 Combat tour, I qualified as a " Master Navigator"!

The rest of the trip, in the new VW, went as planned. We arrived back in Fairborn in time for Alberta's graduation from the University of Dayton on July 30, with a Master of Science Degree, in Counseling.

She, too, had had an eventful and successful year, going to Graduate School to earn her Master's Degree, keeping three children in school, and teaching a Second Grade Class, as well as keeping the home fires burning. By comparison, I had been on vacation.

She emphatically denies any intention to write a book.

POSTSCRIPT

DOWN TO THE ULTIMATE TRAGEDY

The future of South Viet Nam looked optimistic in mid 1967. It and its allies were succeeding in regaining control of the countryside, the Communist forces were being defeated and driven back wherever they chose to fight, and people who had been refugees from the rural areas were being resettled in their hamlets and villages. The local defense units, "Ruff-Puffs", were succeeding in keeping the VC out of their communities. This was known as the Pacification Program.

This kind of success for the people of the South was of course not acceptable in Hanoi. So, a new approach was adopted.

After heavy attacks early in January, the Communists announced a big truce for Tet in 1968. No one would attack anyone during the several days of Tet that year. The Allies accepted the idea, and stood some of their forces cautiously down. But it was not to be. On January 30, the Communists launched full scale attacks all over the country. It became known as Big Tet, the Communist Tet Offensive.

The end result was a military disaster for the Communist side. They lost around 60,000 killed, the Allies a few more than 2,600. Khe San, just South of the DMZ, was the scene of some of the fiercest fighting. The US media made the whole campaign look like an Allied debacle--dead wrong again.

The Allied side did not take advantage by pushing forward. They merely sort of rested, and threw away a good opportunity to prevail.

In spite of their losses, the Communist side managed to launch further attacks in the Saigon area in May, and to draw away some of the Vietnamese troops supporting the rural resettlement programs. These pacification efforts, nevertheless, managed eventually to extend to more than half the rural villages and hamlets.

There never was agreement to proceed with the only sensible military strategy, to take Hanoi.

A complication for the Allied side was that the harbor at Haiphong remained open, facilitating the supply of arms and war materiel to the Hanoi regime, especially from other Communist countries.

Over time, South Viet Nam was able to take over more and more of its own defense, while its allies were able to withdraw more and more of their support. This was called Vietnamization. From a US commitment of nearly 550,000 troops in country early in 1969, the US began bringing men home.

The South Vietnamese government continued turbulent, with changes in Premiers and Presidents. Inflation was a continuing problem, and US financial aid kept the country afloat.

The National Liberation Front, representing the Viet Cong, and the South Vietnamese Government could not agree on any basis for a peace settlement, and peace talks in Paris were delayed.

Ho Chi Minh died in September 1969, but the Communist policies continued unchanged.

The Ho Chi Minh Trail from North Viet Nam ran over into Laos and down through Cambodia, supplying the Viet Cong and the North Vietnamese offensives in the Saigon area. In 1970, a major Allied offensive into Cambodia captured and/or destroyed very large quantities of military supplies brought down the Trail, and then withdrew, by July 1. There were, of course, loud howls of protest, from the media and other liberal thinkers in the US, about what was clearly a defensive action on the part of the US and South Viet Nam.

The Viet Nam Air Force (VNAF) gradually took over more of the air operations of the South's defenses, supplied with aircraft and supported by US training, by the USAF. South Viet Nam's major air training center was established at Nha Trang.

South Vietnamese forces, supported in part by US Air, invaded Southern Laos in an effort to cut off the Ho Chi Minh Trail. The effort was only partially successful, and the North protested the US's support.

During 1971, military units from South Korea, Australia, New Zealand and Thailand were called back home, and US Forces were reduced to fewer than 200,000 by the end of 1971. Total

South Vietnamese forces reached a level of more than a million and a half, continuing Vietnamization.

Improved strains of rice helped increase production in South Viet Nam, so that there was a surplus for export. The North's major producing areas experienced severe flooding, and the South offered to help the flood victims. The North rejected the offer.

Peace talks in Paris continued to be stymied by lack of agreement to even start talking.

An anticipated large scale attack by the North, using more than a dozen divisions, well equipped with armor, began at the end of March, 1972. Once again, supported by US as well as VNAF Air Forces, the South proved its mettle by holding off the attacks, which completely destroyed some cities, and led to more floods of refugees. Bombing of the North was resumed, and its harbors were blockaded. A cease fire of sorts was reached in November. The South and the US proposed an eight point plan in Paris, which the Viet Cong and the NVN delegates rejected the next day. The US B-52 bombing of the North continued, with a break for Christmas, to the end of December. Primary targets were power plants, bridges, and military installations. The SAM's (Surface to Air Missiles) were virtually wiped out.

US forces in Viet Nam had declined by then to about 50,000.

With still no agreement for peace talks at the beginning of January, President Nixon ordered resumption of the bombing of the North. Finally, on January 27, the Communists agreed to negotiate. An agreement was reached by the US, RVN (Republic of Viet Nam), DRVN (the Democratic Republic of Viet Nam) and PRG (Provisional Revolionary Government of SouthViet Nam--Viet Cong), to cease fighting, exchange prisoners and to prepare for free elections in the South.

The Paris agreement provided for an International Commission of Control and Supervision for the South, with representatives from Canada, Poland, Hungary and Indonesia. The members were so divided by political and ideological viewpoints and positions that it was never able to serve as a resolver of disputes. Canada resigned from the Commission and was replaced by Iran.

1974 saw continued fighting in the South, but its economic problems, accompanied by charges of governmental corruption, and political upheaval, contributed to a dim outlook. The government was counting on US financial help for development and for military supplies, but Congress cut the appropriations to much less than hoped for. Inflation was rampant, and the unemployment rate was high.

The North had bargained in Paris for reconstruction aid from the US, and it was agreed to, but with the continued Communist aggressions in the South, the help was denied. Meanwhile, the costs of supposrting the military forces they maintained in the South was a severe drain on the North's economy.

South Viet Nam was hard pressed to continue essential health and economic programs, and to continue supporting its military forces. The US Congress refused to vote additional aid to the beleaguered country, sorely needed for fuel and ammunition, as 1975 began. For the North, that was Opportunity Knocking.

So, early in 1975, the Communist troops began attacking in force, both in the area surrounding Saigon, and in the Highlands. Ban Me Thuot fell on March 13, Pleiku and Kontum on March18, and Qui Nhon on April 1. From there it was an almost classic Blitzkrieg that carried the Red forces on into Saigon.

Tragedy intervened on April 4 when a US C-5 Galaxy, carrying 243 Vietnamese orphans and their adult attendants on the first leg of a flight to the US, crashed shortly after takeoff from Ton Son Nhut, because of improperly secured rear hatches, taking more than 150 lives.

The South's President Thieu resigned, and his Vice-President, Tran Van Huong, was unable to form a government. Huong also resigned after seven days, and turned the government over to retired General Duong Van (" Big") Minh. In a last ditch effort at appeasement, Minh ordered all Americans out of Viet Nam. The city fell on April 30, and the South was surrendered to the Communists by Minh. The new rulers proclaimed a new name for Saigon--Ho Chi Minh City.

Every one who could fled the city. There were US ships and Naval Vessels off shore, and helicopters were lifting people off the US Embassy to the ships to escape the NVN Army. VNAF aircraft of every flyable condition were flown out of the country, quite a number to Thailand. There was one report of a Vietnamese O-1 pilot who managed to load his entire family, six of them altogether, into an O-1 and flew out to a US Carrier for a safe landing, after its flight deck was cleared.

People fled any way they could on boats of all descriptions and sizes, they became known as the Boat People. Many of them were picked up by ships, others became victims of pirates.

The influx of Vietnamese refugees to the United States totalled more than 140,000. They have established themselves as hard workers and loyal citizens. In spite of having to learn a new language, most of the young people have excelled as students in our schools.

The victorious North renamed the country the Socialist Republic of Viet Nam (SRVN). It has fought brief wars with China, Laos and Cambodia. Its introduction of Communism to Cambodia in the 1970's led to the regime of Pol Pot, who brought about the deaths of more than 2,000,000 Cambodians.

Many of the South's leaders, Catholic Bishops among them, were confined for extended periods of time; some were executed.

The present government is trying hard to make Viet Nam a mecca for tourists, and is trying to attract foreign investments, but bureaucratic restrictions and maneuvering make that very difficult. The political disease (Communism) which infected Russia early in the Twentieth Century, and spread so disastrously to Asia, finally was defeated in its original hatching place, due to the skill and determination of Ronald Reagan. But it still continues over a large part of the Earth. Perhaps the rewards of Capitalism will some day cure it.

Meanwhile, I still pray for the ordinary people of Viet Nam, especially for Mama-San and Tanh.

John F. Welch

OTHER BOOKS BY JOHN F. WELCH

DEAD ENGINE KIDS (Editor and Author)
A B-17 Crew's Combat Tour with the Eighth Air Force
Silver Wings Aviation, Inc.*, 1993

RB-36 DAYS AT RAPID CITY (Editor and Author)
Reign of the B/RB-36 at Rapid City/Ellsworth Air Force Base, 1949-1957
Silver Wings Aviation, Inc.*, 1994

VAN SICKLE'S MODERN AIRMANSHIP (Editor and Author)
Compendium of Aviation Knowledge
Fifth Edition, 1981, Litton Educational Publishing
Sixth Edition, 1990, TAB BOOKS
Seventh Edition, 1995, TAB BOOKS

FLIGHT INSTRUCTOR'S POCKET COMPANION (Author)
How to Teach Flight Instructors How to Teach
McGraw-Hill, 1997

FAIT ACCOMPLI (Editor)
History of the 457th Bombardment Group (H), flying B-17's with the Eighth Air Force
Compiled and Published by James L. Bass, 1997

*Silver Wings Aviation, Inc.
2933 Country Club Drive
Rapid City, South Dakota 57702-5218
605-343-4070

My Year in Viet Nam

My Year in Viet Nam